An ESL Ministry Handbook

Contexts and Principles

An ESL Ministry Handbook

Contexts and Principles

Michael D. Pasquale, Ph.D.

An ESL Ministry Handbook

Published by Credo House Publishers, a division of
Credo Communications, LLC, Grand Rapids, Michigan;
www.credohousepublishers.com.

ISBN-10: 1-935391-57-7
ISBN-13: 978-1-935391-57-9

Cover and interior design: Frank Gutbrod

Printed in the United States of America

This book is dedicated to my parents, David and Anne Pasquale,
and my parents-in-law Sam and Damaris Bolet.

My parents have been a great example to teach me
to love others as Christ loves us.
You encouraged my love of learning and were supportive
of my desire to serve in ministry.

My parents-in-law have lived life as immigrants
and second-language learners of English.
Your testimony has inspired me to continue to minister
to those who need Christ.
Thank you for praying for me, even before you knew me!

Acknowledgments

I would like to thank the many people who were instrumental in developing this project, from ideas to written word. I am most grateful to Monica, who has not only been a supportive wife but my ministry partner and closest colleague in the area of ESL ministry. She has read every part of this manuscript and has offered key editorial advice through each stage of development.

Thanks also to the many key people on the publication side of the project. First to my former student Moriah Sharp, who was one of the first to encourage me to write this book. Many thanks also to Shirley Brinkerhoff, formerly of ABWE Publishing. She sadly passed away recently, but she had a key role in offering editorial insight as well. Thanks to Tim Beals and Donna Huisjen at Credo House Publications for help in the last process of publication.

I also want to thank those in faith-based ESL ministry who have shaped and encouraged my thinking on the topics shared in this book. Joan Dungey, my first TESOL professor at Cedarville College, started me on the path to working in ESL ministry. Thanks to Reid Minich and Vicki Ivester at ABWE. Reid especially has been a mentor, encourager, and friend.

Thanks also to those at Maplelawn Baptist Church, Leonard Heights Baptist Church, and First Baptist Church of Lowell who have served as our "home" bases for working and serving in ESL ministry over the years. The ideas presented in this book have definitely gained shape from the years spent working with dear teachers and students at these churches.

I want to thank a few in particular (which is always tricky because it will be impossible to list everyone who has had a positive impact!). I am especially grateful to Keith and Debby Jones, Dr. Mike Sullivan, Rachel Allen, Dr. Jude Fabisch, and Roger and Sandi Weber. Thanks also to the pastors, ministry teams, and ESL teachers at First Baptist Church of Lowell with whom we are currently honored to serve. You have been great examples of living out the principles set forth in this book.

Contents

Introduction

Three Stories About ESL Teachers

Jackie—A Missions Trip to Asia

Jackie walks into a crowded classroom, wondering "What am I going to do?" She smiles nervously as she looks into each of her students' faces, not sure how to read their expressions. Eyes quickly drop wherever she looks. Her heart flutters a little more rapidly, and her stomach tightens as she thinks to herself "I'm not ready for this!" This was definitely not what Jackie had in mind when she signed up for a six-week missions trip to Asia. She knew she was to spend a few weeks helping missionaries evangelize through English outreach classes. But, as a 20-year-old college student majoring in history, not education, she is not prepared to teach, and now that realization floods her mind. "Hello, my name is Jackie." No response. *What am I going to do? Why did I come here?*

Keith—Local Church-Based English Outreach

Keith is also a 20-year-old college student. His major isn't education either, but he has volunteered at his local church to teach in an English outreach class. "I'm not really qualified to teach English," he admitted to a fellow volunteer. "What can I do to prepare myself?" On the advice of this volunteer, he has attended a training seminar and familiarized himself with some basic English as a Second Language (ESL) methodology. He has asked some of the more experienced ESL teachers to help him get together some ideas for lesson plans. It is his first day of class at the church. His lesson is planned, his objective is set, and he is ready to go, excited that he can contribute to this ministry. "Father," he prays silently before the class begins, "please give me opportunities to be a friend to these students so I can share Christ with them." He looks up as the first student enters the room, confident in his purpose, both to teach English well and to be a living example of Christ to his students.

Carol—One-on-One English Tutoring

Carol is a 30-something mom who stays at home raising her two children. She put herself through college working retail and used her office technology degree in her role as an administrative assistant at a small photography studio, where she met her husband George. The couple decided that Carol should stay at home after Scott, their oldest, was born. Six months ago Carol was pulling weeds in the garden when she noticed a family unloading furniture from the back of a pickup truck next door. After a few attempts at striking up a conversation, Carol realized that the adults in the family didn't understand English. Over time she has befriended the young mother, Rosa Santos, but they can only hold conversations through an interpreter, usually one of the Santos children. Today on her mother's behalf Rosita, the youngest of the Santos children, has asked Carol whether she would help Rosa with her English. Carol is taken aback. She would like to help. *But what can I do to teach Rosa English?* Carol struggles with her thoughts. *I don't have any teaching experience. Where do I even begin?*

What links these three stories? Preparation is the key to an effective English outreach ministry. Many people who are involved in such ministries are not formally trained in ESL and are faced with situations similar to those of Jackie, Keith, and Carol.

Who Is This Book For?

This book is primarily for those who are not formally trained teachers yet find themselves with an opportunity to teach English in one of these three ESL contexts: *short-term missions, local church-based classes,* or *one-on-one tutoring.*

Short-term Missions

Short-term missions is defined as temporary contact with another culture, usually lasting from two weeks to a couple of months. It is becoming increasingly popular to send out teams of students or members of a church to a mission field for a few weeks. The short-term context can also include English camps or vacation Bible school programs in the US and Canada that focus on English outreach.

Local Church-Based Classes

Local church-based classes are defined as ongoing ESL classes, usually held in a church building. These are generally weekly classes that continue throughout the year. They are used in the US, Canada, and other countries as a means of community outreach.

One-on-One Tutoring

One-on-one tutoring can occur in varying degrees of formality. Tutoring can take place within an existing class program in order to give students additional help. Often native English speakers are approached and asked to help English learners. These contacts may occur within a church setting or among neighbors. This kind of contact is common on the mission field and has been a great source of bridge building in some regions in which it is difficult to gain evangelistic contact.

What Are the Purposes of This Book?

This book has two main purposes. First, it will prepare you for an immediate need (e.g., orientation for a missions trip, training to teach an ESL class, or help with informally teaching someone English). It will help you prepare ESL lessons, direct you toward valuable resources, and provide a firm background in ESL principles to guide your decision-making.

Second, it is my desire that this book would open up the field of ESL to you. I hope that many of you will want to pursue ESL as a career or ministry option. My prayer is that you will love teaching and reaching others through ESL, with the outcome that you will take more trips or teach more classes. Accordingly, I hope that this exposure will whet your appetite for more training. Perhaps you will be motivated to take a course in TESOL (Teaching English to Speakers of Other Languages) at your local university or to attend a training seminar.

This book is intended to supplement and facilitate the training of ESL teachers in churches, on the mission field, and in similar contexts. Most books dealing with ESL, especially church-based ESL, concern methods—the "how-to"—and lock those who are not formally trained in TESOL into one particular method or curriculum. Many teachers have little knowledge of the vast field of resources outside of that particular context. This book will help teachers develop a personal philosophy of ESL ministry and teaching, equipping them to be principled, grounded teachers, able to tap into numerous resources and to apply them effectively within various contexts.

Some may ask why anyone should be trained for a two-week missions trip overseas. My answer is "Why not?" Thousands of dollars are spent to get just one person overseas and then to house and feed them, etc. If you are going on a missions trip to teach English, what qualifies you for the task? What are you planning to do while you are there? How are you going to go about it? These are all questions that need to be answered, and this book will help you address them.

You want to be effective in your ministry—and to earn the respect of others. But you need to go beyond methods to get to the heart of the matter. Why will you be teaching someone English? Are you going to evangelize? How are you going to use English to do so? There has been increasing scrutiny of ESL methodology from the secular world, with the frequent accusation that many Christian groups are using English classes with a "bait-and-switch" agenda—that churches are offering non-substantive English classes in order to proselytize. Christian organizations are accused of justifying a lack of professionalism as a "means to an end."

Christian ESL teachers need to be excellent in their work. Don't forget that when you travel to another country to teach English, you represent your church, school, or mission agency, as well as your country and Western culture. What you may not realize is that you also represent a profession—the TESOL profession. You need to respect that field and to represent it well. You are not expected to know *everything* (you may opt to get a degree later on or to learn more about TESOL; once you get a taste of it you may very well desire more training). But basic professionalism, respect, and preparedness are imperative.

This principle applies as well to church-based ESL settings in North America. Churches need to provide the services they advertise. If students are not getting what they have come for, they will vote with their feet and not return to the church for classes. Even free classes cannot retain students for long if they do not feel they are successfully learning English. Churches need to be clear on the *why*, the *what*, and the *how* of their intended program before implementing it. Why is your church spending time and money on this program? What is its purpose, and how are you going to go about meeting it? What is your plan?

You will be effective in an ESL ministry when you understand and implement the principles—both ministry and teaching principles—so that you can adopt a personal philosophy of ministry and teaching. This will be a basic statement that will be foundational to the choices you make in curriculum and lesson activities in various ESL contexts. The goal of this book is to prepare you to teach well in any of these specific situations. This book will not teach you all you need to know about TESOL, but it will attempt to point you in the right direction and to orient you within the discipline so that you can further develop as a teacher.

Jackie's Story Revisited

Jackie walks into a crowded classroom and smiles with anticipation—she is about to teach an English class to students in Asia. She is not an education major, but she has recently participated in a seminar for English teachers to help her prepare for an ESL class. She worked on her lesson plans before leaving for Asia and then consulted with the lead teacher for a final review. She is nervous but confident, hoping that by the end of her six-week stay in Asia she will have been able to help her students significantly with their English. She breathes a silent prayer: "Lord, thank you for this opportunity. Help me to develop trust with these students, with the longer-term result that they will also build trust with the missionaries. Give all of us opportunities to share your love."

Chapter 1

ESL Ministry Principles

What Is a Principle?

A principle is a fundamental truth or quality about a particular subject. Organizations often talk about "guiding principles"—organizational qualities that help administrators and group members make decisions. In this chapter we will discuss relevant ministry principles that can guide an ESL teacher when making decisions within any of the three ESL contexts examined in the introduction. Chapter 2 will cover the principles of teaching. We will see how ministry and teaching principles go hand-in-hand and how an understanding of these principles will help you to apply them effectively in an ESL ministry. They will guide your decision-making in such areas as which curriculum to use, how to approach a particular lesson, or how to develop an ESL program. They will help you choose the format of your program and which activities to include.

In order for these principles to be effective, they need to be focused and memorable. My goal is that when you reach a crucial point—when a student asks you a question, when you need to make a quick decision about a class activity, or when you are pressed for time creating a lesson plan—that you will be able to easily recall and apply these principles.

Principle #1: Be Ethical

Both Christian and non-Christian groups have to varying degrees charged those involved in ministry-based ESL with unethical behavior. There are two basic accusations, the first of which is lack of preparation and standards for teachers. Many organizations spend very little time training their teachers, with the result that these teachers do not teach with quality. The demand for ESL teachers is so great that native English speakers are highly sought after, regardless of their degree of training or experience. Christian mission groups and churches want to seize the opportunity to fill this need and reach people for Christ. But too often, in a rush to provide classes, they neglect thorough teacher training.

An ESL ministry that displays a good ethic is one that provides adequate training for both the teaching and the ministry aspects of the program. Those coordinating church ministries or leading short-term missions trips need to include training as part of their preparation and ongoing support of their volunteers. They can either provide the training themselves or invite an expert, such as a professor from a local college or a teacher in a community ESL program, to do so. They should in addition provide periodic in-service training, orient teachers to new materials, and provide them with information about other training opportunities, such as professional workshops and conferences.

Ethical ESL teachers take it upon themselves to acquire training, whether or not their program structure makes it available. Those who have no teaching background or experience can benefit from learning basic education methods, while those who already possess teaching skills can delve more deeply into specific, specialized ESL theory and methodology. Teachers who want to be proactive in increasing their knowledge and skills can take advantage of opportunities like local conferences, quality reading resources (see recommended reading lists at the end of each chapter), courses at local universities, or opportunities to be mentored by experienced teachers.

The second charge leveled against Christians using ESL as ministry is a lack of transparency in terms of the motives when Christian teachers use ESL as a tool to evangelize. There are two aspects to this criticism. First, critics contend that Christian teachers should be open and explicit from the outset about their desire to evangelize. Second, critics accuse churches of using ESL classes with a "bait and switch" agenda. Churches advertise an English class, but the curriculum is centered more on evangelism than on academics. They are concerned that Christian teachers in this situation use the classroom not primarily to teach English but to promote a hidden agenda of proselytizing.

As for the first aspect, it is critical in all circumstances that teachers conduct themselves with integrity. Those who accuse Christians of a lack of transparency demand "full disclosure." They seem to be implying that Christian English teachers should stand up in front of the class on the first day and announce, "I am a Christian. My purpose is to evangelize you." I disagree with this approach. My contention is that while it goes without saying that we need to be honest and transparent, we don't necessarily have to take this approach. We shouldn't let others define us. We should be able to clearly present the message of Christ and what real Christians are like. It is important for us to recognize in the first place that the word "Christian" means different things to different people. In many parts of the world "Christian" refers to any Western person and carries an immoral connotation. Therefore, we need to be intentional in defining who we are, making certain our students understand what we mean by the word "Christian."

As for the second aspect, I would argue that evangelism and discipleship are legitimate goals of any ministry-oriented ESL class. Still, it is imperative that churches deliver on what they have promised. If churches advertise an English class, they need to provide just that. Furthermore, they should provide the highest quality English class they can with the personnel and resources available to them. As representatives of Christ in the world, how could the church do any less? It is our obligation as Christians to keep our promises. According to Jesus, we who are of the kingdom of heaven should be so transparent that we simply let our "yes" be "yes" and our "no" be "no" (see Matthew 5:37a). In addition, Christians can gain the trust of their students only by delivering on what they promise. Only when they do so will Christians be able to develop relationships with their mentees and hope for the opportunity to share Christ with them.

Principle #2: Be Hospitable

As Christians teaching in a ministry setting, we have a desire to lead students to Christ. How do we make the leap from the initial goal of teaching English to the ultimate goal of seeing students come to know Christ and grow as Christians? These two aims are not mutually exclusive, and as a matter of fact they are both necessary. As we have seen previously in this chapter, we must be excellent English teachers in order to be ethical and to earn the respect and trust of our students. Further, we must invest in people's lives and build friendships in order to share the gospel and to mentor and disciple.

Why is hospitality needed? Suppose that, instead of an ESL ministry, we are providing food for the homeless. If we allow each person to come into the church, go through the line, and then sit alone to eat, the individual might recognize that the food has been graciously provided by the church but experience no personal interaction. On the other hand, what if church members make it a point to sit at each table and enjoy food and fellowship with whoever sits down to join them? What if each person being served is advised that the church families at their table have provided the meal especially for them? Only then do they see love manifested in service.

The reality is that love is at the center of hospitality. What if your neighbor needed food? That need could be met by advising them about the availability of free food at a nearby food bank. But a more hospitable approach would be to invite them over for dinner and then offer to take them to the store for more groceries—personal touches that would serve as an investment in their lives. You are not only helping them but getting to know them, a vital first step in evangelism and discipleship.

The overarching characteristic of hospitality is love. How we display love in an ESL setting will vary according to the context of the ESL ministry. In a classroom situation, time for fellowship can be built into the schedule. Perhaps there could be a 15- to 20-minute break in the middle of the class period with drinks and treats provided. This could either be an informal time for small talk or a slightly more structured exercise with general conversation topics provided by the teacher. This is a good way for volunteers from the church who are not teachers to become involved in the ministry, and it serves other purposes as well. Academically, it provides a low-pressure atmosphere in which the students can practice their English. It also furnishes a good opportunity for church members to get to know the students. Other ideas for discussion are theme parties (such as a Christmas or Valentine's Day party), other cultural activities (perhaps a Fourth of July picnic with fireworks), or field trips (to local museums, the zoo, or even the mall). Again, these activities offer both academic benefits and relationship-building potential.

In order to show God's love to our students on an individual level, we need to be sensitive to the students' needs. When a need is expressed, either overtly or indirectly, we are to be ready to meet it or to direct the person to someone else who can. Of course, no one person will be able to meet the needs of everyone in the class. Perhaps the church can maintain a list of members willing to provide car rides, for example, along with a schedule of their availability. In this way many can share in the task of providing transportation, in the effort of building relationships, and in the joy of seeing people grow and change.

Another way in which hospitality can be tangibly expressed is in our attempt to acquire the language of the people we are trying to reach. While this is certainly helpful within a classroom situation, it can be even more powerful within the contexts of one-on-one relationships or short-term missions trips. In the classroom teachers are inherently viewed as authority figures. In the other two contexts, by trying to learn the others' language we are in a sense putting ourselves on the same level as those to whom we are ministering. This shows that we value them and their culture and also makes it clear that we are not asking them to lose their cultural heritage and identity by learning English. In addition, this effort on our part can go a long way toward equipping us to empathize with the struggles of learning another language.

For those participating in short-term missions trips, this is not optional. It is imperative that the volunteers learn at least some functional phrases in the language of the host country. This is important for practical purposes ("Where is the bathroom?" "I'm lost. Where is the American embassy?") and also shows common courtesy to our hosts. We need to enter into their setting in an attitude of humble service, not egocentric overconfidence.

Let's return to Carol's story to illustrate hospitality in action. Carol was approached by her young neighbor Rosita with a request to teach English to Rosita's mother, Rosa Santos. Carol began meeting with Rosa one or two times a week, at first moving slowly through a picture dictionary to work on vocabulary items. Carol was glad she could help by giving English lessons, but she felt that there wasn't much of a connection between the two of them. Carol then decided to start listening to Spanish tapes during the day. After a few weeks Carol saw Rosa leaving the house in the morning.

"Buenos días" ("Good morning"), she called, recognizing that she was speaking with an accent and feeling a little sheepish. But Rosa smiled broadly and returned her greeting. Carol continued practicing some simple Spanish phrases with Rosa when she saw her. Carol was aware that she made mistakes, and sometimes Rosa couldn't help but smile. But a bond was being created between them. Rosa would help Carol with her Spanish and Carol would reciprocate by helping Rosa with English. Carol also babysat the Santos children when Rosa needed to go to a doctor's appointment. The two women built a bridge of friendship over the course of many months.

One day Carol and Rosa were chatting over a cup of coffee after the English lesson. There was a pause, after which Rosa looked up and observed shyly, "Carol, you so nice to me. Why you different from other neighbors?" Carol's heart leapt and she quickly breathed a silent prayer. This was the chance she'd been waiting for!

Principle #3: Be Prayerful

It may seem obvious to state that we need to pray in ministry, but the truth is that we often neglect prayer in much of our daily lives. We may work hard, be excellent teachers, use the best and most current methods, and show love to our students. But unless the Lord works in their hearts they will never come to Christ. In Jesus' words, "No one can come to me unless the Father who sent me draws him" (John 6:44a). As a matter of fact, without God's working "there is no one who understands, no one who seeks God" (Romans 3:11).

Prayer is vital in all contexts of ESL ministry. It helps us to maintain focus and to become the excellent teachers we want to be. When we are attuned and sensitized through prayer to the Lord's leading, we are enabled to display love and hospitality. It is essential not only that we pray as individual teachers but that we also incorporate group prayer in our preparation. To personalize Paul's words in Ephesians 6:18–19, we ought to "pray in the Spirit on all occasions with all kinds of prayers and requests." With this in mind, be alert and always keep on praying for all who are involved in the ESL ministry. Pray for each teacher, that whenever they open their mouths, words may be given them so that they will fearlessly make known the mystery of the gospel.

On an individual level, we must pray for our own students. Spend time getting to know your students by name and becoming aware of any needs you could pray for. Pray for their ability to learn English and to do well in the class. Pray that the students will be motivated to return to class. And, of course, pray for their spiritual needs. It is easy to segment our busy lives so that we neglect to think of our students outside the classroom setting. By praying for each one on a regular basis, we keep them in the forefront of our minds and hearts.

Those who will be traveling as part of a short-term missions team can begin to pray for their future students before they leave on their trip. Continue to pray for your students while you are in the country, as well as after you return home. It is relatively easy to remember to pray for those you meet while the excitement of the trip is fresh in your mind but much more of a challenge to continue to pray for those you have met but no longer see. If possible, keep in contact through e-mail or by exchanging postcards on a regular basis. This will not only give your students a chance to practice their English but will help you remember them when you pray. You will also be made aware of current prayer needs through continued correspondence.

The local church can play a crucial role in sustaining and supporting an ESL ministry. This support should go beyond monetary help to include regular, earnest prayer from the whole congregation. ESL ministry, whether conducted at home or abroad, is doing the work of the Great Commission. Volunteers need prayer support from their local churches in order to make that happen.

When the ESL ministry begins, as well as at certain natural transition points, such as the beginning of a new semester, the pastor can give the teachers a "commissioning" service and pray for them in front of the congregation. This is also a great idea for short-term missions teams before they travel. The weekly ESL class should be on the prayer bulletin for prayer meetings.

A member of the ESL team could provide updates during the services as part of a brief missions update. Those who are working on a less formal, one-on-one basis can include prayer requests on behalf of their students on the church prayer list and in other settings, such as Sunday School or small group meetings. Each of us needs God to help us as we minister. Above all, we need to pray that our students will come to accept Christ as their Savior and grow in Him.

An ESL Teacher's Prayer

Lord, thank you for this opportunity to serve You.
Please help me to think clearly and to communicate well with my students.
May I be prepared and display excellence in all that I say and do.
Please help me to love my students. May I be an encouragement to them.
I pray that they will see Christ in me.
Give me boldness and wisdom to seize any opportunity to share Jesus with them.
May my students come to know You as their Lord and Savior.
Amen

Summary

It is critical for teachers to gain their students' trust. This may be accomplished through teaching with excellence (i.e., being ethical) and demonstrating your genuine love for them (i.e., being hospitable). The power to do this comes through diligent prayer. We will discuss principles of teaching in Chapter 2.

Ministry Principles

Be Ethical
Be Hospitable
Be Prayerful

For Further Study

Pasquale, Michael, and Nathan L. K. Bierma. *Every Tribe and Tongue: A Biblical Vision for Language in Society* (Eugene, OR: Pickwick Publications, 2011).

Smith, David I. *Learning from the Stranger: Christian Faith & Cultural Diversity* (Grand Rapids, MI: Eerdmans, 2009).

Smith, David I., and Barbara Carvill. *The Gift of the Stranger: Faith, Hospitality, and Foreign Language Learning* (Grand Rapids, MI: Eerdmans, 2001).

Snow, Donald. *English Teaching as Christian Mission* (Scottdale, PA: Herald Press, 2001).

Chapter 2

ESL/EFL Teaching and Learning Principles

The Importance of Simple and Memorable Teaching Principles

While the ministry principles presented in Chapter 1 primarily focused on the role of the teacher within an ESL context, the teaching and learning principles underlying this chapter are student-centered. Since my approach to the material centers on you as the teacher, however, there will be no need for you to make this distinction on an ongoing basis or to determine precisely how the student-based principle in any given part of the discussion relates to my comments to you as teacher. These principles, based on current second-language acquisition (SLA) theory and methodology, are simplified and discussed in plain English so that they can be easily remembered. When you are in a teaching context that requires an immediate decision, you can rely on your knowledge of these principles.

This chapter covers four basic ESL teaching and learning principles, which together can be summarized from the teacher's side as: *Be prepared to teach the ABCs.* The teacher must *be prepared* for each ESL session, understand the students' ***a****ttitude* or motivation for learning English, encourage them to ***b****e diligent* in study, and encourage them to ***c****ommunicate* in English.

Principle #1: Be Prepared

The first principle mirrors the ministry principle of being ethical: *Be prepared* to teach. The importance of being prepared for each class or tutoring session cannot be overstressed. This does not necessarily mean that everything needs to be planned out to the minute, but class objectives must be clear.

Any uninitiated person is at least a little nervous before teaching a class. Being prepared goes a long way in helping you overcome that apprehension and direct your energy into teaching the lesson.

The best way to prepare for a class or session is to write out a lesson plan. We will discuss different kinds of lesson plans that can be used for a formal ESL class or an informal tutoring session.[1] The key component is having a primary focus or objective for your class time.

Formal Lesson Plans

A formal lesson plan can be divided into five parts: *the class objective, review, teacher presentation of new material, student practice of new material*, and *homework.*

Formal Lesson Plan

Date

Class

1) Class objective:

2) Review:

3) Teacher presentation of new material:

4) Student practice of new material:

5) Homework:

Formal lesson plans also allocate an approximate amount of time for each section of the class period. A good overall length for a class session is between one hour and ninety minutes. This gives enough time to cover relevant materials without being too long for either the teacher or the students. A ten-minute break can be figured into a ninety-minute class.

Class Objective

The first section, the class objective, indicates the main focus for the class period. It will guide you as the teacher in terms of materials, illustrations, activities, and homework ideas. Your class objective should be clearly stated and specific (avoid generalities like "Today we will learn about nouns and verbs" or "We will learn English today"), as well as realistic and achievable. This is particularly important for beginning students, who cannot take in too much new information. Even if the focus is simply presenting new vocabulary words or numbers, limit new vocabulary in a lesson to ten or fifteen items. More advanced courses can cover more ground. Good class objectives for a beginning-level class might be "Students will learn a basic greeting exchange" or "Students will learn vocabulary words related to food preparation."

Review

The second section of the lesson plan deals with the way you will begin your class session, quite possibly with a review of previously covered vocabulary and grammar. It is always good to review at the beginning and end of each session, as repetition is key to information retention. If you mention something only once or twice and then move on to the next item, your students will not remember it well. A simple tip to keep in mind is that the more your students use their five senses—the more they see, touch, smell, taste, and hear (actually or figuratively) during the course of the lesson—the more likely they will be to internalize the information. For example, you can review vocabulary words using the visual aid of flash cards with pictures, or you can read a story that contains the words and grammatical structures you have presented.

Presenting New Material and Student Practice

The next two sections will account for the bulk of the lesson time. First you will present new vocabulary words, English grammatical structure, or a cultural situation to your students. Then your students will practice using English associated with the lesson. These components will all be related to the main objective or theme listed as your class objective. During the lesson time it is usually more effective to work on several short activities connected around a theme rather than to stretch out one long activity. For example, you can spend fifteen minutes reading a story and then have students work in pairs for another fifteen minutes to complete a questionnaire related to the story. This can then be followed by a group reading, a role playing activity, or computer work.

It is important that you assign homework, especially within the context of a formal class. The work does not have to be "required" or even graded, but it will give students direction for using English outside of class. We will talk more about the importance of homework in the discussion of Principle #3. The homework assignment can be simple, such as a written or audio journal entry. This is an especially good idea for homework during a short-term trip or for a one-on-one experience, as it requires very little preparation and few materials.

Informal Lesson Plans

Although a teacher can use a formal lesson plan for all English-teaching contexts, it may be more practical and time-effective to write an informal lesson plan if you are tutoring a student one-on-one or are involved in a conversational English camp or class. An informal lesson plan still has a basic theme or class objective. Perhaps you will work through a newspaper story together or go over words related to a doctor's office. Just have an idea of what you will cover and the materials you will need.

Flexibility

Always keep in mind the importance of flexibility. Sometimes it is better to forego your lesson plan and "go with the moment." This is particularly true if the class or conversation goes into a more spiritual direction. If a current news event sparks interest in discussing the Bible, by all means talk about the news event and its relation to God's Word! Perhaps a student has a serious personal problem and wants to talk. It is certainly all right in this context to skip the prepared lesson and minister to your student.

Also, within the course of a class period or lesson you may find it advisable to change the direction of the class or to stop doing a particular activity. Perhaps your students are finding the activity to be too difficult or too easy, or you have an extra ten minutes of class time. Be flexible! Always be prepared with extra activity or reading ideas. It is advisable to create an ESL "toolbox" with materials to help you in your class, along with activity ideas and props. If you are involved in a church-based program, it would be a good idea if each classroom were equipped with a toolbox. However, all teachers can create their own personal toolboxes. One suggestion is to use a hanging file folder box with a handle on top. This enables you to maintain separate files of lesson plans and pictures, along with space for materials.

ESL Toolbox Ideas

- Flash cards (e.g., numbers, letters, vocabulary words)
- Play money
- Magnetic letters and words
- Pictures / paper dolls / finger puppets
- Small toys (e.g. animals, cars, trucks, etc.)
- Maps
- Picture dictionary
- ESL dictionary (simplified English dictionary for your students)
- Foreign language-English dictionary
- Pens, pencils, crayons, markers, etc.
- Calendar
- Children's story books
- Magazines

The general rule for Principle #1 is to prepare yourself through formulating a lesson plan. Following are some examples pertaining to the contexts we are discussing. For a church-based ESL class, Keith will prepare a formal lesson plan for his beginning-level students, a plan that might go something like this:

October 15th class at Community Baptist Church

Beginning-Level Class

Objective: Students will learn four English prepositions (in, on, beside, under)

Review (10 minutes): Vocabulary words from last week (box, ball, put, etc.)

New Material to Be Presented (15 minutes):

- Write the four prepositions (in, on, beside, under) on the board.
- Give students four cards with each preposition written on one of them. Have students pick up the card with the preposition I read.
- Bring in a shoe box and a tennis ball. Review the words "box" and "ball." Demonstrate how the ball is "in the box," "on the box," etc.
- Write on the board "The ball is ____ the box." Fill in and demonstrate with ball and box. Have students write down each sentence.

Students Practice New Material
(20 minutes + 10-minute break before reading time):

- Have a student come to the front of class. Point to the sentence and read it aloud, filling in one of the prepositions (e.g., "The ball is in the box"). Have the student demonstrate the sentence with the ball and the box.
- Review the verb "put." Write the sentence "Put the ball ____ the box." Point to the sentence and fill in one of the prepositions, such as "Put the ball in the

box." Have the student demonstrate the sentence with the ball and the box.

- Have two students come up. One will point to / say a sentence, and the other will do the action.
- Have students read the story passage and underline all instances of the prepositions being studied.

Homework: Have students bring in something with one of the prepositions written on it (e.g. a newspaper article, a box of crackers, etc.).

If Carol were to teach the same material to Rosa, she could write a note to herself that she would like to teach prepositions such as *in, on, beside* and *under* and that she could use props such as a ball and box to demonstrate. She could also make a note to bring along pictures to teach or review vocabulary items and then to use those pictures to teach the new prepositions. For example, if Carol had a picture of a cat and a dog sleeping together, she could review the words "dog" and "cat" and then say "The cat is beside the dog." Carol could also use materials in Rosa's house by walking around and saying things like "The lamp is on the table." These are just a few general examples of how to write and use lesson plans. Chapters 4 and 5 will provide more detailed information.

Principle #2: Attitude

You can remember the next three principles by thinking about the "ABCs." The "A" is important as you prepare for a class. Why do your students want to learn English? Do they need to prepare for a school exam? Do they need to survive in a new country? Do they want a better job? Do they just want to meet new English-speaking friends? The answers to these questions will determine how you will prepare for your class, what curriculum you will use, and how you will keep interest high. One method for determining student interests is to hand out a questionnaire on the first day of class. This is especially important for a formal class situation. A structured program could begin with a registration day where people sign up, take placement exams, purchase their books, etc. If the teachers know, for example, what topics students want to study ahead of time, they can more effectively prepare for the term.

All teachers want their students to be highly interested in the course material, enjoy coming to class, do their work with excellence, and willingly complete all assignments. This is often an unrealistic expectation, however, especially when applied across the board to all students. The reality is that some will enjoy the course material and the way you teach, while others will not. The key is to feed off the encouragement you receive from the productive students rather than allowing yourself to become discouraged by those who do not seem to care about the course or are critical of your teaching methods. You cannot please everyone, and even the best teachers have students who do not do well in their classes.

Positive Attitude

The attitude of students in a class is important, but it is seldom uniform. You will want to try to create a positive attitude in your class by being aware of your students' cultural backgrounds and what they expect from you as a teacher. Bear in mind that what is accepted in one culture is not necessarily considered appropriate in another. It is common now in American schools for teachers to be informal in order to relate better to today's youth culture. However, as an ESL teacher you should maintain a more conservative approach, both in dress and in teaching style, so as to not offend your students. Of course, this will greatly depend on which cultures your students are coming from. I would for example encourage teachers to lean more toward the conservative side with students from a Muslim culture, while being more relaxed with younger students from Western cultures. The key issue is to understand your students and try to maintain a positive atmosphere in the classroom. In terms of your desire to make a positive first impression, remember that dress and teaching style have great impact. Your sustained focus on course topics will be another important factor for determining student interest in the course. It is imperative that you as a teacher be aware of student needs and attuned to the level of interest.

Let's look at another illustration, using Jackie's short-term missions trip to Asia as an example. Her preparation should include asking the missionary contact in the host country questions about her teaching situation, such as the ages of the students. How many will be in the class? Do they all come from the same language and cultural background? Why are these students taking an English course? How much English do they already know?

In many cases the answers to these questions will not be uniform. You may find yourself teaching a class with a wide range of students in terms of age, cultural and/or language background, and English proficiency level. Jackie learned that she would be teaching a group of high school students who wanted to prepare for the TOEFL (Test of English as a Foreign Language) or the IELTS (International English Language Testing System) exams. The TOEFL exam is primarily used to test the proficiency of students wishing to study in the US, while the IELTS exam is used by the British Council to test students who want to study in the British Commonwealth.

In order for Jackie to encourage a positive mindset in the classroom, she would need to show her students that her lesson plans would specifically help them prepare for their exam. She would focus more on reading and writing than she would in a basic, conversational English class. She would also spend time reviewing more advanced vocabulary words that might be used in academic settings. Again, understanding *why* a student is taking the course is very important to course planning and preparation and, accordingly, can go a long way toward ensuring a high level of student interest and retention.

Realistic Expectations

It is critical that both students and teachers have realistic expectations about learning English. It is easy for students to grow discouraged when English does not come easily or their accent still makes it difficult for others to understand them. In a short-term setting this is especially important. If you will be working with students for just two or three weeks, you will want to adjust your expectation level, accepting the reality that only a little progress will be made. Even a short-term class can lead to significant progress in the long run, but a student will not jump from being a beginning student of English to becoming an advanced student with only a few hours of class work. A good rule of thumb for an ESL course is to cover a little material and teach it well. Focus on a few main grammar points or semantic areas (e.g., vocabulary and discourse rules related to ordering food in a restaurant), and be well prepared. For their part, students must work hard, thereby building a strong foundation for further language development. They too will benefit from learning only a little material but learning it well.

Principle #3: Encourage Students to Be Diligent Learners

The next principle specifically relates to what your students will need to do to become successful English learners. It is critically important that they *be diligent learners.* Learning another language is a difficult business and takes time, and it is imperative that you stress this to your students. According to language learning expert Dr. Stephen Krashen, it takes three years of intensive language learning, on average, to function well in an English-speaking community.[2] Another report in *TESOL Quarterly* estimates that it will take between five and seven years for an ESL student to catch up with peers who are native English speakers.[3] One factor that can help accelerate this process is the willingness of a student to work hard both in and outside of class. Independent work is essential to gaining fluency and proficiency in a foreign language.

Independent Work

What can you as a teacher do to help? One suggestion is that you make clear to your students that you view homework as an essential part of your class or tutoring program. Students can practice their English by writing in a journal.

- A student can write on topics you provide for them, especially those that relate specifically to the class session.
- Students can also write about English language issues or items they come across in everyday life. They can work to become more aware of the written and spoken English around them.
- They can write about a newspaper article they read or a television program they view. Students can comment on signs and English-language advertisements they see. Students can do this even in non-English-speaking countries. They may come

across English-language advertising, see an English language newspaper, or avail themselves of access to CNN or the British Broadcasting Channel.

- The Internet is another good source of English language material.

The next essential activity in which your students should be involved is reading. Several research studies have shown a direct link between extensive reading and the acquisition of a second language.[4] Interestingly, parallel studies also show that children acquire their first language faster when they read.[5]

There are a few important keys to making reading most effective. First, the material should be easy enough so that a student will not have to look up many words in a dictionary. Fluent reading is the key. It is important for students to come to understand words through context, just as native speakers do. The text could be a little challenging, but they must understand a majority of the material, not just the gist, for the reading to be beneficial.

Second, the reading material should be enjoyable and interesting to the student. Some people enjoy reading a newspaper because they like learning about current events. Others prefer the sports pages or an entertainment magazine. Beginning students can read children's books. The material does not have to be "academic" in order to be useful. As a teacher, encourage your students to read. If you are able, take them to the library or make books available to them in your classroom. If you are going on a short-term missions trip, bring along some small and inexpensive books to give to your students. You can donate old books you are no longer using or purchase books at a used or a bargain bookstore. If you are tutoring a student one-on-one, you can read a book together and talk about it. You can even offer a Christian book to be used as a witnessing tool. I have used easy-reader Bible stories as a discussion starter in a church-based ESL class.

One final point is that different students learn differently. Some prefer a more "hands-on" type of learning and enjoy group projects, role playing, etc, while others respond to a more methodical approach, preferring to see the grammatical structures worked out on paper. One method is not necessarily better or more correct than another. What is important is that your students determine what works best for them and then work hard. If a student finds it helpful to study verb conjugations, then it is fine for them to look at a grammar book on their own time. Another student may prefer to watch a video with English subtitles. The key to extra work is that it be effective and enjoyable. If students do not enjoy an activity they will not stick with it. One way or another, reading will help students immensely, whether they prefer comic books or classic works.

Principle #4: Encourage Communication

The third component of the "ABCs" is to help your students *communicate* in English. It has been shown that learning a second language is more effective when students are interacting with the language and learning to communicate with it, not just learning the grammar and vocabulary.[6] It is important that you encourage your students to communicate in English, both in and outside of class. In fact, this is one of the most important things they can do for themselves in preparation for thinking, speaking, and writing fluently in English. The key is to get students comfortable enough with the language to practice, accept mistakes, learn from those mistakes, and eventually respond "automatically" in English. Students show fluency when they can produce English sentences automatically, without having to translate from their first language. (Chapter 4 offers practical tips on teaching students to listen and speak in English.) The principle here is that students learn best when they use English in action.

One aspect of learning to communicate is to *understand the context* in which the language is being spoken. It is much easier for students to learn a new language when they can connect the words and phrases to a particular time or context when it might be appropriate for them to use them. Language is best learned in its natural context. This can be done in an "immersion" setting in an English-speaking country; this gives an advantage to those who teach English in the US or Canada. If possible, take your students out into the community and surround them with English. You can bring them to a supermarket and show them products and packaging written in English. Students can practice asking questions of native speakers in unique environments.

While it may not always be possible or practical to take students out into a natural setting to learn English, a teacher can recreate an English-speaking context within a classroom. Simply by using pictures or creating a role play environment, you can expose students to English being used in its natural context. Students can also interact with video or computer programs that demonstrate the use of English in context. It is very effective for students to move beyond seeing the printed word to seeing and hearing the words used by native speakers in a particular setting. Following this model, students can practice using those language forms in context.

The "Silent Period"

Be careful to balance encouraging students to communicate with avoiding excessive pressure to do so. You want your students to be comfortable enough to take risks in using the language but not so intimidated that they will "shut down" and refuse to use the language at all. Krashen talks about a "silent period"[7] that parallels the way a child learns its first language. A baby can understand and react to language months or even years before being able to produce intelligible utterances. In the same way most students learn a second language best when they are allowed a period of time to digest the language without pressure to produce sentences.

It is important to bear in mind, though, that just because students are silent does not mean that they cannot communicate or must remain passive learners. You can and must encourage your students to communicate and interact with the language by such means as pointing or using gestures, signs, or flashcards with words. Another good tool to use is an interactive computer program such as *Rosetta Stone*.[8]

Comprehensible Input

Another key principle of communication is that the *kind of input* (spoken and written examples of the second language) *is just as important as the amount of input.* If all it took to learn a language were listening to massive doses of input, many people would become bilingual just by watching a Spanish channel on television. The key is access to what linguist Stephen Krashen calls "comprehensible input"[9]—input that is understandable by a student. For example, if you review vocabulary words with your students before they read a story that contains those words, that story will be more understandable to them than a story with unfamiliar words. Input can be given in many ways.

- A teacher can speak in the second language.
- You can give the students vocabulary words with corresponding pictures.

- As mentioned earlier, reading is a great source of input for students.
- Students can also listen to CDs or cassette tapes in English. They can follow along and read a story while hearing it on tape. Activating two senses at once, in this case hearing and seeing, is always a great way to increase input.

While we easily remember to speak more slowly and clearly in the presence of others who are not proficient in our language, we also need to remember to use language our students can understand. In many cases relying on nonverbal cues will not be helpful, since students may smile and nod even if they do not understand. It is critical to keep checking for comprehension. Ask questions. Have your students repeat and review key material. As the saying goes, practice does indeed make perfect!

Communication in Context

The last key aspect, an important one, relates to how we want our students to communicate. We want them to keep grammar in its proper context and to know how to communicate competently within a proper cultural context.

The teaching of formal grammar in English classes has been deemphasized over the last thirty years. As a result, many native English speakers do not understand basic grammatical terms such as "modifier," "conjunction," and "appositive" until they themselves are in the process of learning a foreign language. It is helpful for you as a teacher of English to understand grammatical terms, since they will be used in textbooks and many of your students will be aware of them. It is not required, however, that you be a grammar expert in order to teach English. Whenever we teach English we are teaching "grammar," since we are teaching students about the parts of the language (e.g., the words and parts of words) and how to put those pieces together (e.g., how to construct a sentence in English). It is helpful for you to be able to identify a "subject" and a "predicate," but you do not need to use those terms with your students. If a student has an overtly grammatical question, you can take the time to look up the answer in a grammar reference and share that information at a later time.

There was a time when foreign language classes exclusively focused on grammar and taught students how to translate sentences back and forth between their first language and the language they were learning. Very little, if any, cultural background was provided. Many students came away from such classes assuming that all one has to do to learn another language is to translate their first language into the second. The reality is, though, that a language cannot be separated from its culture easily, if at all, so a student must learn how to communicate in cultural situations. This *communicative competence* involves more than just grammatical knowledge (i.e., *linguistic competence*); it is the ability to *use* that language within a particular context.

For example, students need to understand how to greet someone in English, a task that includes more than just the words or grammar. This involves, for example, the ability to differentiate between greeting someone in a formal situation and greeting a friend. If there is a cultural difference involved in greeting someone of the opposite gender, students need this information. Conversely, teachers need to know if such a distinction is operative in the home culture. Culture and language are in a case like this intimately connected. Other areas that should be covered in an ESL class are appropriate and acceptable ways to apologize, to accept or decline an invitation, to answer the telephone, to ask for something, etc. These issues are of practical importance to learners of English, who need to know *how* to communicate in addition to *what* to communicate.

This last principle, *communicate*, covers a lot of ground. Learning to communicate in English should be the primary goal of an English class.

- We need to be aware of our students' need to understand us, and we need to provide them with plenty of English input.
- We need to be deliberate about placing language within grammatical and social contexts.
- We also need to encourage our students to communicate even if they are not yet ready to do so verbally.

If you put this last principle into action, you will see your students becoming more comfortable communicating in English. This can be accomplished through a formal class, a short-term missions trip, or a one-on-one tutoring session.

Summary

Teaching and Learning Principles

Be prepared to teach the ABCs

Be prepared ...

Understand a student's **attitude**.

A student must **be a diligent learner**.

A student must be encouraged to **communicate** in English.

Key Ideas:

Repetition is the key to retention.

Students should use several senses when learning a language.

Be flexible.

Prepare an ESL toolbox.

Students and teachers must be realistic in their expectations.

Students should read extensively in English.

Cover only a little but teach/learn it well.

Perception precedes production.

Keep grammar within its proper context.

Students need to be communicatively competent.

Notes

1 There are many Web resources available to provide lesson plans and worksheets for ESL classes. Some popular ones include using-english.com, esl-galaxy.com, and learnenglishfeelgood.com.

2 Stephen Krashen's model for teaching foreign languages was presented in two books:
Principles and Practice in Second Language Acquisition (Oxford:

Pergamon Press, 1982) and *The Input Hypothesis* (London: Longman, 1985).

3 Virginia Collier. "How long: A synthesis of research on academic achievement in a second language." *TESOL Quarterly*, 23 (1989), 509-531.

4 The case for extensive reading (or "Free Voluntary Reading") in second language classrooms was made by Richard Day and Julian Bamford in *Extensive Reading in the Second Language Classroom* (Cambridge: Cambridge University Press, 1998). See also Stephen Krashen, *The Power of Reading* (Englewood, CO: Libraries Unlimited, 1994).

5 W. E. Nagy, P. Herman, and R. C. Anderson. "Learning words from context." *Reading Research Quarterly*, 20 (1985), 233-253.

6 James Asher in *Learning Another Language Through Actions*, 6th ed. (Los Gatos, CA: Sky Oaks Productions, 2003) introduces the teaching model called "Total Physical Response" (TPR). TPR will be covered in Chapter 4.

7 Stephen Krashen. *Principles and Practice in Second Language Acquisition* (Oxford: Pergamon Press, 1982).

8 *Rosetta Stone* (Harrisonburg, VA: Fairfield Language Technologies).

9 Stephen Krashen. *The Input Hypothesis* (London: Longman, 1985).

For Further Study

TESOL Methodology:

Brown, H. Douglas. *Teaching by Principles: An Interactive Approach to Language Pedagogy*. 2nd ed. (White Plains, NY: Pearson Education, 2007).

Celce-Murcia, Marianne, ed. *Teaching English as a Second or Foreign Language*. 3rd ed. (Boston: Heinle and Heinle, 2001).

Doff, Adrian. *Teach English: A Training Course for Teachers* (Cambridge: Cambridge University Press, 1988).

Second Language Acquisition Theory:

Ellis, Rod. *Second Langauge Acquisition* (Oxford: Oxford University Press, 1997).

Gass, Susan M., and Larry Selinker. *Second Language Acquisition: An Introductory Course*. 3rd ed. (Mahweh, NJ: Lawrence Erlbaum Associates, 2008).

Lightbown, Patsy M., and Nina Spada. *How Languages are Learned*. 3rd ed. (Oxford: Oxford University Press, 2006).

Chapter 3

Developing a Personal Philosophy of Teaching Statement

What is a Personal "Philosophy of Teaching Statement"?

A "philosophy of teaching statement" summarizes a personal vision of teaching. As such it provides the sense and purpose of teaching from the standpoint of the individual instructor, articulating the personal values that underlie the why and how of teaching for him or her. A philosophy of teaching statement will flesh out, in your own words, what your goal is for teaching and how you will go about accomplishing that goal. The ministry principles in Chapter 1 and the teaching and learning principles of Chapter 2 will form the basis of your statement, which will then guide you as you choose materials and methods of teaching (Chapters 4 and 5) as they relate to listening, speaking, reading, and writing. Think of your personal philosophy of teaching statement as your foundation for future classroom choices in curriculum and methodology.

Why Do I Need to Write a Philosophy of Teaching Statement?

You may question why you would need to write a philosophy of teaching statement, especially if you are only participating in a short-term missions trip. The reality is that you need to ask yourself why you are going to teach English (and to travel thousands of miles and spend thousands of dollars to do so). Once you can answer the *why*, you need to address the *how*. How are you going to go about teaching English? It is important for you to think through the previous two chapters and to express your thoughts in your own words. Your philosophy of teaching statement does not need to be lengthy; in fact, a short statement will be better since you will be more likely to remember it. The key is to personalize these principles for your particular *context* (e.g., formal class, missions trip, one-on-one setting) and *situation* (e.g., in a church, in a school, in a foreign country, etc.). Socrates once reflected that "the unexamined life is not worth living."[1] In a similar way, it may be said that an unexamined task is not worth doing. Contemplation is not in vogue in our busy lifestyles today, but we need to take the time to prepare our minds for a task such as teaching English, especially if this endeavor is aligned to ministry outreach.

How Do I Write a Philosophy of Teaching Statement?

You have already completed the first step in preparing your philosophy of teaching statement by reading and engaging with Chapters 1 and 2 in this book. These chapters gave you the ministry principles (*be ethical, be hospitable*, and *be prayerful*) and the teaching and learning principles (*be prepared to teach the ABCs*) that will be the foundation of your philosophy of teaching statement.

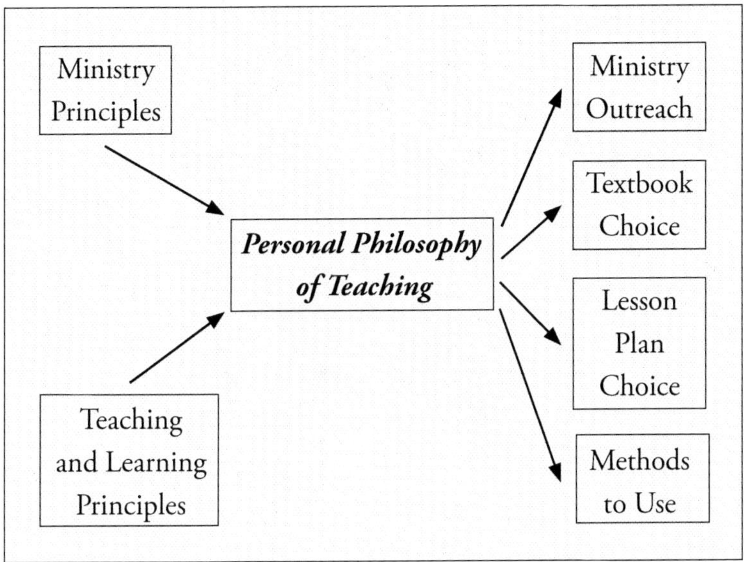

Once you have reviewed and thought through those principles, making decisions as needed, you are ready to begin writing. I want to pause at this juncture and stress that contemplation must be accompanied by prayer. Let your heart be moved by the Spirit so that your instruction will be done from a spirit of compassion for those you are going to teach. Ask the Lord for opportunities to use your knowledge of English teaching for His glory.

Two main areas will be at the heart of philosophy statements based on the principles in this book—seeing students come to know Christ better (i.e., salvation and discipleship) and helping students learn English.

"Philosophy of Teaching Statement"—Two Main Sections:

How am I going to minister to my students?

How am I going to teach my students English?

Each statement will focus on these main areas, while reflecting your personal situation and teaching style. For example, someone teaching in a formal school setting may be required to follow a particular curriculum in class. This restriction may mean that you as a teacher have to prepare for classes and teach for seven or eight hours a day. The main emphasis in this scenario will be on teaching students to learn English well. This does not preclude involvement in sharing Christ, but the philosophy statement will have to be adapted to fit the particulars. You as the teacher may in this case be able to build friendships with students after class or over lunch.

On the other hand, a one-on-one tutoring session may be primarily a Bible study or discipleship time, with a less formal emphasis on English teaching. A philosophy statement for this situation would differ greatly from the first. I invite you to look with me at a few examples of teaching philosophy statements written by the teachers we introduced in the previous chapters: Jackie (short-term missions trip), Keith (formal class in local church), and Carol (one-on-one tutoring with neighbor named Rosa).

Examples of Philosophy of Teaching Statements

As a part of a team from her university completing an orientation program that will cover cross-cultural communication, some language acquisition, and general team-building activities, Jackie is preparing to participate in a summer missions trip to Asia. The missionary family in Asia has sent an e-mail to the team leader, giving her an idea of what to expect during the summer. Each team member will be teaching an English class to be held at an English camp. The Asian students will be taking English lessons in order to enhance their communication skills in order to prepare for their college English exams. A major emphasis of the camp experience will also be recreational. The missionaries will be providing opportunities for ministry outreach during the weeks of camp. Jackie will be teaching English four hours a day to the same group of students, most of whom are about her age. They already have a solid grasp of English grammar but lack the communication skills needed for fluent conversation. Jackie's teaching philosophy statement is written as a prayer, while still covering the two main areas: how she is going to minister to her students and how she is going to teach them English.

Jackie's "Philosophy of Teaching Statement"

Summer Missions Trip to Thailand; Intermediate to Advanced Students

Lord, you know I am preparing to go on a six-week missions trip to Thailand this summer. I feel so inadequate but pray that you will help me! I am preparing myself for this task by reading and going over the curriculum given to me by our team leader. I want to be used by you, Lord, this summer. I want to see my students touched by the Spirit. Lord, please help me. I don't even know the names of my students yet but am praying for each one right now. Prepare them for the classes, giving them clear minds and a willingness to talk and take communication risks. I pray that any student who does not know you will see Christ through my example. May they accept Christ!

Keith prepared himself for teaching his ESL class by reading books on language teaching and attending seminars at a local university. He understood that his classes would be more formal, traditional English classes and accordingly focused on how he would teach English effectively. He wanted to be sure that the methods he used in a classroom would encourage his students to communicate well in English.

Keith worked with the program administrator to understand what kinds of students he would have in his classes. The questionnaires revealed that his class would be made up of eight students, all of whom were beginning learners of English. Three of his students had Bosnian as a first language, and the other five spoke Spanish. Their ages ranged from the 40s to the 60s. He understood that his students would expect a fairly formal class and was prepared to meet their expectations. He also knew that the underlying reason for having ESL classes at his local church was ministry outreach. He wanted to make sure to learn about his students and take an interest in their lives. He planned to make a prayer list of his students' individual needs and to pray daily for each of them. Keith's teaching philosophy statement was more structured, reflecting the more formal nature of his class.

Keith's "Philosophy of Teaching Statement"

Community Baptist Church; Beginning-Level ESL Class

What am I going to teach?

My focus will be to encourage my students to communicate in English. They will need a strong foundation in English vocabulary and discourse skills. Important grammatical structures will need to be covered sequentially.

How am I going to teach?

Each class will provide opportunities for my students to communicate in English—both orally and in writing. I will assign regular journaling assignments and encourage my students to be diligent in writing on a daily basis.

Why am I going to teach?

First, I want to see my students become more comfortable in speaking English in order to become a more integral part of our community. Second, I will pray for each student regularly, asking that they will accept Christ as their Savior or, if they are already believers, that they will grow as disciples of Christ. I will be prepared with topics for reading and discussion related to Christian themes.

Carol has been tutoring her neighbor, Rosa, for a few weeks and wants to be better prepared for these English lessons. Rosa wants to learn English so that she can communicate with her children's teachers at school. She also wants to be able to use the telephone to make appointments and the like. Carol's philosophy statement is written as an essay.

Carol's "Philosophy of Teaching Statement"

I see teaching English to Rosa as a way to reach her with the gospel. Rosa has a lot of practical needs with regard to language, such as speaking with her children's teachers and making appointments on the phone. I want to help her communicate effectively in these kinds of situations. When we meet for coffee each week, I will make sure to cover areas of English that Rosa will need in order to live and function in the US. I also passionately want to see Rosa and her family come to know Christ. I want to model Christ's love to her and be her friend. I will pray for her and her family. Ultimately I want to see Rosa become more comfortable in speaking English, as well as to accept Christ as her Savior! I would love to continue her English lessons as a discipleship class too! I need the Lord's help to do this well.

Summary

A "philosophy of teaching statement" is your personal guide to teaching an ESL class or lesson. It can take any of several different forms, depending on your context and situation, among them a question-and-answer format like Keith's, an essay like Carol's, or even a written prayer like Jackie's. Any form is acceptable as long as it helps you to remember the ministry, learning, and teaching principles so that you can apply them to your particular situation.

Steps in Drafting a Personal "Philosophy of Teaching Statement"

1) Pray.
2) Review ministry principles (Chapter 1) and teaching/learning principles (Chapter 2).

3) Briefly describe your teaching context (e.g., formal classroom, short-term missions trip, or one-on-one tutoring) and situation (e.g., in a school, in a church, in a foreign country, etc.).
4) Write out in your own words *why* you want to teach English in your particular context and situation.
5) Write out in your own words *how* you are going to go about teaching English in your particular context and situation.

Notes

1 Plato *Apology*, 38; Plato, *Five Dialogues*, translated by G. M. A. Grube, p. 41 (Indianapolis, IN: Hackett Publishing Co., 1981).

For Further Study

Brookfield, S. *The Skillful Teacher* (San Francisco: Jossey-Bass, 1990).

Chism, Nancy. "Developing a 'philosophy of teaching statement.'" *Essays on Teaching Excellence*, 9(3), 1-2 (1998). Professional and Organizational Development Network in Higher Education.

Chapter 4

Teaching Skills in Listening and Speaking

An Overview

This chapter shows you how to apply the ESL teaching and learning principles of Chapter 2 to the teaching of listening and speaking. By using your philosophy of teaching statement as a guide, you will understand how to use various techniques and resources to help students improve their perception and pronunciation of English.

This chapter offers tips and suggestions for teachers in each of the contexts we have discussed—a church-based classroom, a short-term missions trip, and one-on-one tutoring. It includes ideas for simple assessment strategy and placement tests, in addition to illustrating some of the ideas for a "toolbox" discussed in Chapter 2 and introducing some "power tools" to help you teach listening and speaking skills. You could use the ideas presented in this chapter to plan your own curriculum and lesson plans. The chapter also points you in the direction of many helpful resources; a list of suggested resources is included at the end.

Listening and Speaking

Foreign-language methodology textbooks often focus on the "four skills" of learning a foreign language: listening, speaking, reading, and writing. These four skill areas are not mutually exclusive, but they work together to characterize what we mean by "language competence." When a student is learning English or another foreign language, he or she will follow certain stages toward a greater understanding of and proficiency in the language. First, a student will gain greater understanding of the spoken language, comprehending much more than he or she is able to produce. As stated in Chapter 2, "perception precedes production." Once students begin to understand more vocabulary, phrases, and grammatical structures, they will begin to produce those words, phrases, and structures with increasing confidence. This chapter focuses on listening and speaking because these two skills work closely together and form the foundation for beginning-level instruction.

After a foundation has been built from understanding the spoken word and being able to communicate orally, reading and writing skills can be developed. All of these skills are closely connected, of course, and cannot be completely separated from one another. For example, reading basic words can be a part of the introductory process, along with writing simple words and phrases. Chapter 5 will cover in more detail the areas of reading and writing, dealing with how a student can come to read longer and more complex passages of text and develop as a writer. This will progress from writing sentences and phrases to formulating complex clauses. The discussion will also address writing according to context (e.g., how to formulate a business letter versus writing a personal e-mail).

Be Prepared to Teach

Whether you will be teaching in a formal classroom setting or an informal situation, preparation is key. One of the basics you will need to understand is what kind of class you will be teaching. Is improving English conversation the main focus? Or is the class a more formal academic course or tutoring arrangement geared toward teaching English grammar and composition? Once you know what kind of class you will be teaching, you will need to find out how big your class will be, at what level (or levels) your students are functioning, what native language (or languages) they speak, and what resources will be at your disposal.

Conversational Classes

A class or small group labeled "conversational" has at its center an atmosphere that promotes listening and speaking comprehension. Conversational courses taught by non-academically trained teachers are common, since the draw for students to this kind of class is their desire to be able to talk and interact with native speakers of English. Teaching a conversational class can look deceptively easy to a casual onlooker, but it is imperative for an instructor to be as prepared for this as for any other class. A teacher in a conversational class must be prepared with discussion topics and understand how to skillfully direct a conversation. It is best to try to involve as many students as possible in talking and sharing. If a conversation group is meeting in conjunction with a formal class, the discussion topics can be based on the lessons covered in the main class.

Class Size

Preparation includes knowing how many students you will have. This is not always possible, especially in an ongoing church-based program where the number fluctuates. In general, however, knowing how many students to expect will help you plan for the class. In a smaller group a teacher can use a more "hands on" approach with all of the students. A conversation could plausibly include everyone in the group, allowing the teacher to monitor the progress and participation of each student. In a larger class several groups of students would need to be established, with the teacher floating from group to group to participate in or monitor the conversations.

An advantage of having small, student-led groups is that it forces students to take the initiative in using English instead of relying on the teacher to facilitate the flow of conversation. A disadvantage in a class with many shy or quiet students is that it becomes difficult to maintain small group conversations. Often these groups will transition from English into their native language, so it is important for the teacher to try to keep the groups on track. For ongoing classes, attempt to establish groups of students that include a good mix of extroverts and introverts. It is important to have conversation times no matter what size your class is, from large, formal classes to intimate, one-on-one settings.

Know Your Students

Another important aspect of preparing for a class is to know the proficiency level of your students. This initial assessment can be done through a formal placement test or by using informal strategies. In the contexts covered in this book it is fine to use informal assessment strategies. A church program may hold a registration day or administer tests on the first day of class. If a program has an open enrollment policy, the test may be given on the first day of each student's arrival. In that case it may be best to have one person or a team of people designated to administer the test so that the other teachers may begin their classes on time.

An assessment test should cover the four basic skill areas of listening, speaking, reading, and writing. Chapter 5 will cover the assessment of reading and writing. A good strategy to use in testing listening and speaking is to ask the student a few questions like "What is your name?" or "Where are you from?" The answers to these questions will not only help you get to know the students but will aid in your awareness of how much they already understand and can say in English.

Appendix C includes assessment guidelines to help you test language proficiency. In general, the better the student can understand and produce English sentences, the higher the level of class that student can enter. As a matter of practicality, if you do offer different classes for beginning-level to advanced-level students, you might want to allow your students to choose for themselves what level of class they will attend. Some students prefer to start at a slower pace and refresh their knowledge and use of English, so they may initially attend a class that is perhaps a bit too easy for them. Others will want to be challenged and will place themselves into a more advanced class from the outset. Either way is fine if there is a choice. However, if a student is struggling after a time or does not seem to fit well into a particular class, you may want to suggest an alternative placement.

In order to get a full picture of a student's proficiency in English, all four skill areas must be tested. Some students will test higher in some areas than others. For example, if a student is taking a conversational English class, their proficiency in listening and speaking may be advancing faster than their reading and writing skills. On the other hand, in a formal English class setting a student's knowledge of grammar and writing in English may progress at a faster pace than their spoken communication skills.

Know Their Languages

The fourth aspect of preparation is to become aware of what native languages your students speak. It is easier to teach a class in which all students have the same native language. This is especially true when teaching pronunciation skills. Speakers with the same native language will make similar "mistakes" when speaking English (we can, for example, recognize a "French" accent because native French speakers pronounce English in a systematic way, based on how their native language influences their perception and pronunciation). This principle is true of every language. There are some sounds that are easier for some and more difficult for others. Some of the resources listed in Appendix B will help teachers handle specific pronunciation issues with certain languages, such as helping Japanese speakers pronounce the English sounds "l" and "r."

A class with several native languages represented presents some challenges, but, as has been said, "Variety is the spice of life!" Obviously it is easier to plan for a class if everyone has the same starting point. This also relates to having multiple levels of students in the same class. In both cases you must try to find a balance between going too slow or focusing on only one language group and trying to make progress in the class as a whole. You may need to rely on the stronger students to help the weaker ones. In multi-language classes, groups of students with the same language can be paired together to work on assignments specifically geared toward their needs. On the other hand, it may be beneficial at times to split up students so that their small groups are comprised of a variety of language speakers. Sometimes the most challenging situations can also be the most rewarding. When you are faced with a particularly challenging situation, remember to be flexible and to do the best you can with the situation that presents itself. How often isn't it true that when we are stretched we see God doing some amazing things!

The ESL Toolbox

Finally, it is important for you to prepare your ESL toolbox for teaching both speaking and listening skills in your classes. This will include preparing file folders that contain ideas for listening and speaking lessons. It is important for every good ESL teacher to have a ready stack of pictures to use in class. Pictures cut from old magazines and newspapers can be great conversation starters. A picture truly is "worth a thousand words," and for an ESL class it can be worth a productive fifteen-minute speaking exercise!

If you will be participating in a short-term missions trip, prepare a small folder that contains pictures of objects, people, and situations. Also be sure to include pictures of your own family, your pets, and other universally interesting subjects. These can help not only in leading conversations but also in building relationships with students.

An indispensable tool is a picture dictionary (available in monolingual and bilingual editions). If you need a quick lesson idea, pull out your picture dictionary and make that the centerpiece of your teaching. A picture dictionary is organized thematically, with each page representing a context or situation. For example, a particular page may have pictures of common household items, along with their labels in English. Another page might picture a grocery store or the post office, again with many objects labeled in English. For beginning students, you can either say a word and have them point to the picture or ask them to repeat the word and point. More advanced students can explain what is happening in the picture. Or you might want to tell a story based on what you see in a picture and have your students either finish it or write their own story.

Basic, low-tech classes can use items like a picture dictionary or other props the teacher brings into the classroom. In situations where technology is available to the teacher, a simple tape recorder or CD player might be used to play a story or song. A good listening exercise is for students to listen to a story on tape and then answer comprehension questions, either orally or in writing. If students have access to their own tape recorders, they can prepare an audio journal. Audio journals will be explained in more detail below, but the general principle is to help a student practice English pronunciation. A list of key resources is included at the end of this chapter.

Understand a Student's Attitude

It is impossible to read the mind of every student in order to figure out what makes them tick. There are a few things, however, that are particularly helpful for you as a teacher to know as they relate to a student's attitude or motivation for taking your class. One main question is "Why do my students want to learn English?" and a related question is "Why do they want to take this class with me?" A third question specifically associated with listening and speaking may also apply: "Why is it difficult for my student to try to communicate in class?"

Why Do Students Want to Learn English?

It is important to know why your students want to learn English. This will help not only in your course planning, as we have already discussed, but will also aid you in understanding your students' levels of commitment to the task at hand. In many cases you may have a class of similar students—e.g., those who are learning survival English or are preparing to take an exam. In other cases your students will present you with a variety of reasons for wanting to learn the language. In my experience the most popular reason given for learning English, both by students here in the US and those abroad, is a general desire for self-improvement, often related to such factors as wanting to get a better job, make new friends, or attend college.

Conversational English classes are popular throughout the world. They provide a place for students to improve their conversational skills in English and are more practical in orientation. Students who have a desire to obtain a better job or to learn survival English have a great deal of intrinsic motivation in this kind of class, whereas students who were expecting a more academic-style class may feel disappointed in not learning about verb conjugations or through lectures. Is your class advertised as being conversational, academic, or a little of both? It is important for you as the teacher to clarify the nature of the material and the approach in order to eliminate any misconceptions at the outset.

Why Do Students Want to Take an ESL Class with You?

As we have discussed, it is helpful to have new students fill out a registration form to clarify what they want to learn and to prioritize topics they hope to have covered. Some students will come to your class because they saw an advertisement or heard about it from their friends. Others will come because your class is offered at the most convenient time and/or place or because of cost factors (free in many cases). One lesson teachers learn quickly is that it is impossible to please every student all of the time. Some students will love your teaching style and curriculum, while others will hate it. It is difficult not to take criticism personally but also vitally important for you to understand what you are offering as a course (including the intrinsic limitations of the program) and to try your best to meet the needs of your students. Some will visit and never return, while others will become faithful students. Understanding the individuals' reasons for wanting an English class will help you to more effectively prepare for the class itself, as well as to interact meaningfully with students on a personal level.

Why Is It Difficult for Students to Communicate?

A third vital area to understand is why it is difficult for some students to communicate in class, especially in a conversational setting. The concept of a "silent period" was introduced in Chapter 2, and it is worth reiterating that not all students will be immediately comfortable communicating in class. This may be due to a combination of factors, possibly including an introverted personality or particular factors related to their cultural background. We must be careful not to force students who are not ready to talk; we need to tread carefully in many situations.

Try to understand the class demographics. What are the cultural backgrounds of the students? Does your class consist of both men and women? In approximately equal number? How old are your students? What is the educational background of your students in their first language? All of these issues can be analyzed to determine whether and how much you should encourage your students to converse in class. Many students are uncomfortable with the prospect of making mistakes or of looking foolish to the other students. Culture plays a big role in this situation. A male student, for example, may feel a high degree of pressure surrounding the possibility of making a mistake around those who are younger or around women. Those who are well educated in their home country may feel frustrated at being unable to articulate their thoughts well.

One suggestion for you as a teacher is to initiate a silent period into your class—especially in a beginning-level setting—so that students do not feel compelled to communicate verbally for the first few class sessions. Students can communicate through gestures or by pointing to pictures until they are comfortable enough to speak. Remember that listening and speaking work together. It is helpful for students simply to listen to English being spoken and to witness conversations in action. Once they are able to digest these situations, you can begin to encourage verbal communication. Some students may still feel hesitant in speaking. Encourage them to try, doing all you can to create a warm environment in which they are not ridiculed or laughed at for making mistakes. As students gain confidence, they will begin to speak English with increasing proficiency.

Encourage Students to Be Diligent Learners

Learning a language takes time, and it is imperative that students be diligent learners even outside of the classroom. This is especially true if teachers meet with their students only once or twice a week. Daily interaction with English is necessary in order to gain proficiency. The Foreign Service Institute (FSI) of the US Department of State has listed the approximate number of hours needed to gain proficiency in speaking and reading.[1] For a native speaker of English to learn to speak and read a language closely related to English (e.g., French or Spanish) would require about 575 to 600 class hours over a period of 24 weeks. For learning a language that has significant linguistic or cultural differences from English (e.g., Russian and Zulu), the requirement would be almost twice as long—approximately 1100 class hours over 44 weeks. Languages that are considered exceptionally difficult for native English speakers, such as Arabic, Mandarin Chinese, and Japanese, would take approximately 2200 class hours over 88 weeks. Reversing the direction, we can apply these statistics to the teaching of English and see, for example, that a native speaker of Japanese would need about 2200 class hours to become proficient in English. If we count the number of class hours in a typical college foreign language class (which is about 36 weeks long, at 3–5 hours a week or 108–180 hours a year), we can readily determine how many academic years of study it would take for a student to reach a level of proficiency in even the languages most closely related to English, such as French or Spanish.[2]

What can a student do on his or her own to increase listening and speaking proficiency? Beginning students must expose themselves to the language in a variety of situations over an extended period of time. In light of the reality that "perception precedes production," students must be able to hear and understand the language as it is spoken before they are able to produce clear and understandable English themselves. Options for listening already mentioned include listening to the radio, television, and/or books on tape. In countries where these resources are scarce, teachers may have to tape themselves reading short stories and then distribute the tapes to interested students. The Internet is another good resource for audio materials, as well as, of course, the written word. Radio stations offer streaming audio or archived programs, and both National Public Radio[3] and the British Broadcasting Corporation[4] offer a variety of programs in English. Children's programming is also a good resource for students. Wholesome Christian programs such as *Adventures in Odyssey*[5] and *Down Gilead Lane*[6] are available online and can be a good catalyst for discussing Christian themes and the gospel.

An audio journal is another great tool for your students to use to practice their speaking. A student will need a tape recorder and tape in order to construct an audio journal. In some situations students can use the Internet and, using a microphone, construct a webpage with audio files. Whatever your situation, encourage your students to make an audio journal. This will be most effective if they add an entry each day; they should spend about 15 to 20 minutes just recording themselves. This will be especially helpful for those students who are timid in a classroom environment because it offers them control over the situation and allows them to speak in a "safe" environment. You can provide students with a guide for their audio journals, such as a topic to talk about or a passage for them to read aloud. Encourage your advanced students to play back their journals, listening for areas in which they can make improvements on their own.

Audio journals are helpful only if students are willing to use them to practice their English outside of class. Teachers who are more daring or who want to work on improving students' pronunciation can use these journals to measure the students' speaking progress. It is a good rule of thumb to focus on one aspect of pronunciation at a time (e.g., the pronunciation of "th" or the correct use of the articles "the" and "a"). Teacher comments should be as positive as possible and refer only to the one area that you were listening for. It can be gratifying to go back to early tapes of your students in order to note just how much they have improved in their English pronunciation.

If students want to improve their English pronunciation, it is imperative that they work on this aspect of their speech outside of class. As a teacher, you will need some familiarity with phonetics in order to help with pronunciation. In addition to encouraging use of an audio journal, teachers can focus on teaching specific English sounds in class. Particular sounds will be easier or harder, depending upon a student's native language. A good Internet website on phonetics will include audio examples in addition to a written explanation. The University of Iowa maintains a helpful phonetics website for learners of English, Spanish, and German.[7] It includes videos of a native speaker pronouncing each sound, followed by examples of that sound used in words. This free website would be good for students to use either on their own or in a language lab in which the teacher and student work with it together.

Once again, it is key for students desiring to gain proficiency in English to invest time outside of class. Homework is a vital part of this process, and you as a teacher must help direct their out-of-class learning. Students need to avail themselves of these opportunities and invest the time needed to gain fluency and confidence.

Encourage Communication

The last teaching and learning principle covered in Chapter 2 was that of encouraging students to communicate. Communication is obviously at the center of developing both listening and speaking skills. This section will cover two "power tools" that can be added to your ESL toolbox—the teaching methods called *Total Physical Response* and *Jazz Chants*. These methods are considered power tools in that they are time- and labor-intensive for both teacher and student. However, if they are used correctly, they can produce excellent results in both listening and speaking.

Total Physical Response

Total Physical Response or *TPR* is a method of teaching a foreign language that was developed by Dr. James Asher of San Jose State University in the 1960s. Asher's hypothesis is that adults can learn a second language in a way similar to young children acquiring a first language. Beginning-level TPR focuses on the use of simple commands and directions that students follow without saying anything. This is the "silent period" in action! Just as children are able to understand a great deal before being able to produce sentences, adults learning through TPR can comprehend spoken English commands and perform those actions without having to speak.

Results can be seen immediately, even in a beginning-level class. TPR is a great method to use in a classroom setting in which the teachers do not understand the students' native language and the students do not know English. Through miming and demonstrating while speaking English, students can pick up the meaning and gain a foundational knowledge of the language. TPR can even be fun! A language class using TPR involves a lot of activity and movement, far from the "dry and boring" atmosphere often associated with a foreign-language class. Asher's main idea is that "when the body moves, the brain remembers."[8] Physical response to an oral command will help the student remember the foreign language better. Here is an example of a classic TPR command sequence.

Beginning-Level TPR Example

Number of students: 1–4 (the rest of the class can watch and learn through observing),

Setup: A row of 2–5 chairs that face the class, with the teacher sitting in the extra chair.

Procedure:

(1) The teacher says clearly in English "Stand up." While speaking, the teacher also demonstrates the action by standing up. If the students don't imitate the action, the teacher will need to motion for them to stand up.

(2) The teacher then clearly says in English "Sit down" and then sits. Students should also follow and sit down.

(3) The procedures are repeated several times until the teacher feels confident that the students have heard and understand the words and the corresponding actions.

(4) The teacher can test the students by saying "stand up" and "sit down" without also doing the action. The students should be able to do the actions after hearing the oral commands.

(5) The teacher can expand the lesson by introducing new words or phrases, such as "walk" and "turn around," and by using adverbs like "quickly" and "slowly."

TPR is a good activity with which to develop students' listening skills, as well as a way to actively communicate without needing to say anything. TPR can be used in intermediate- and advanced-level classes as well. Those lessons can include grammar, speaking, reading, and writing. Following is an example of an advanced TPR lesson that includes all four aspects. This sequence, if taught outside the United States, could be part of a lesson on American food customs, or it could be adapted to food customs in the host country.

Advanced-Level TPR Example

"How to Make S'mores"

Number of students: Whole class can participate in groups of two or three.

Set up: Graham crackers, chocolate bars, and marshmallows.

Procedure:

(1) The teacher stands in front of class and says "I am hungry" (teacher can pat stomach to show hunger). "I am going to make s'mores."

(2) The teacher says the following and mimes each action (these are only suggestions; feel free to adapt or add according to your particular situation):

- I take a graham cracker.
- I put on some chocolate.
- I put on a marshmallow.
- I put another graham cracker on top.
- I sit down and eat the s'more.
- This tastes so good!

(3) Have two or three student volunteers come to the front of class and tell the class that these students will now make s'mores.

(4) Give the directions to the students, waiting each time for their response before going on to complete the sequence of commands.

(5) Repeat the series of commands with other groups of students, while the rest of the class watches and learns.

(6) One or two volunteers could also say the commands to the ones making the s'mores.

(7) The teacher now writes the list of commands on the board.

(8) As writing practice, students can copy down the list of commands in their notebooks.

(9) Students can then practice giving the commands to a partner.

(10) More advanced students can write out new commands or even a story based on these commands.

(11) For reading practice, point to a command on the board and have the students respond by reading it aloud. (You may want to mix up the order of the commands on the board.)

Jazz Chants

TPR is a tool to help students listen, but as we have seen it can also be used to develop the other areas of skill. Another "power tool" that can help students with speaking is called *Jazz Chants*. Jazz Chants were developed by Professor Carolyn Graham, who has taught at Harvard and Columbia Universities. She uses music and rhythm to help students learn to speak English with the correct intonation. The original Jazz Chants books have spawned numerous sequels, including *Small Talk, Grammar-chants*, and *Holiday Jazz Chants*. She has also helped produce Jazz Chants for children, including a series featuring Clifford, the Big Red Dog. The *Small Talk* book is especially good for beginning-level students because it helps them learn how to greet people, apologize, and develop other very basic skills.

The *Grammarchants* book includes exercises to help students understand English grammar, such as differentiating between "the" and "a" or between "he" and "she" or practicing use of the comparative "-er" and the superlative "-est" with adjectives and adverbs. Jazz Chants are particularly effective in that students can both hear the tape (or the teacher can read the chants) and respond. Music helps make the lesson enjoyable. A teacher must use discernment, however, being aware of the possibility that certain chants may offend some students. This does not invalidate the concept but just means that you should review any chant before using it. For example, you may want to avoid the chant "Shh, Shh Baby's Sleeping" because it contains the line "shut up, shut up, baby's sleeping!" You can even write your own chants to use in class. Following is an example of a chant I have used.

Jazz Chant Example

"Introductions"

1) Teacher should go over new vocabulary words, such as *hello, day*, etc.
2) If there is no music background tape, or if you are making up your own chant, have the class clap in rhythm.

3) The teacher says the first line, such as "Hello, hello."
4) The class repeats the line: "Hello, hello."
5) The teacher says the second line: "Nice to meet you, nice to meet you."
6) The class repeats "Nice to meet you, nice to meet you."
7) The teacher says the third line: "How are you today?"
8) The class repeats "How are you today?"
9) Teacher: "I am fine."
10) Class: "I am fine."
11) Teacher: "Have a nice day!"
12) Class: "Have a nice day!"
13) Have students work in pairs, each taking turns being the leader and the repeater.
14) Teacher should review all vocabulary words at the end.

As indicated, Jazz Chants are effective because music and repetition help students to remember them, and adult students should not feel awkward using music in class in this manner. Jazz Chants have been used in top universities around the world, including Harvard and Oxford. In fact, Carolyn Graham originally conceived of Jazz Chants as a way to teach adults and only later applied her work to children.

Dr. Joan Dungey of Cedarville University has applied the Jazz Chant concept to the teaching of English with the Bible. She has written a book titled *Gospel Chants*, which includes chants that simply recount stories from the Gospels, such as that of Jesus walking on the water or the story of Zacchaeus.9 The chants can be used in conjunction with the teaching of the Bible story, and the session can include an English lesson that reviews the vocabulary words and grammatical structures.

Summary

The teaching of listening and speaking is foundational for effective student communication in English. Teachers need to teach slowly and deliberately, helping students in a nonthreatening manner to gain greater confidence and proficiency in speaking the language. Power tools such as TPR and Jazz Chants can help add spice to any class session, while at the same time helping students increase proficiency in listening and speaking. Once a firm foundation has been set, students are ready to blossom into reading and writing.

Notes

1 Foreign Service Institute, www.state.gov/m/fsi; see also National Virtual Translation Center, www.nvtc.gov/lotw/months/november/learningExpectations.html.

2 Ibid.

3 National Public Radio, www.npr.org

4 The British Broadcasting Corporation, www.bbc.co.uk

5 *Adventures in Odyssey*, Focus on the Family, www.whitsend.org

6 *Down Gilead Lane*, Children's Bible Hour, http://cbh.gospelcom.net/gilead

7 University of Iowa Phonetics website, www.uiowa.edu/~acadtech/phonetics

8 James Asher. *Learning Another Language Through Actions*. 6th ed. (Los Gatos, CA: Sky Oaks Productions, Inc. 2003).

9 Joan M. Dungey. *Gospel Chants* (Yellow Springs, OH: R & J Productions, 2004), www.eslbible.com

For Further Study

Total Physical Response:

Cirafesi, Wally. *English in Action: A Fast and Fun Way to Learn English*. 4th ed. (Colorado Springs, CO: Dawson Media, 2001). Student and teacher editions.

Garcia, Ramiro. *Instructor's Notebook: How to Apply TPR for Best Results*. 4th ed. (Los Gatos, CA: Sky Oaks Productions, 2001).

Jazz Chants:

Dungey, Joan M. *Gospel Chants: Language Practice in a Call and Answer Format* (Yellow Springs, OH: R & J Productions, 2004).

Graham, Carolyn. *Jazz Chants* (Oxford: Oxford University Press). With audio CD.

Chapter 5

Teaching Skills in Reading and Writing

An Overview

This chapter shows you how to apply the ESL teaching and learning principles of Chapter 2 to the teaching of reading and writing. The emphasis is on the teaching of reading and writing, and it includes a focus on grammar, with suggestions on how to cover grammatical issues in class. This chapter includes lesson illustrations and sample activities and incorporates a special focus on using the Bible in ESL lessons.

Reading and Writing

The skills of reading and writing are both activities and processes. For example, "reading" can be as simple as seeing a series of letters, such as "c-a-t," and recognizing those letters as representing an idea or word. Some students are skilled enough to be able to "read" a sentence (sometimes flawlessly) without comprehending its meaning. Reading is a skill that can be developed. We can teach students, for example, to read to understand the gist of the sentence and later work with them on mastering some deeper concepts, such as finding the main idea, locating specific information in the text, understanding the organization of a paragraph or story, and even predicting what will happen to the characters or ideas within the story.

Writing is a similarly complex skill. Students can copy down simple words or write their name, progressing with time to learning how to piece together words to form simple, compound, and complex sentences or to effectively formulate a paragraph. Students then need familiarity with the different genres of writing, such as a business letter, a personal note, an academic essay, an e-mail, or a shopping list. A fuller understanding of grammar is necessary, but this is also, at least to some degree, developed by students through the process of learning to read and write. A student may be able to communicate with words and short phrases in speech but must also come to understand how to construct a complete English sentence in writing. Reading also enhances the students' grasp of English grammatical structure.

Be Prepared to Teach

In a certain sense, teaching reading and writing takes more preparation than teaching listening or speaking. A student—and especially a beginning-level student—must be led to a reading or writing task with care. For example, key vocabulary words and cultural contexts need to be explained before assigning a reading passage. Similarly, some grammatical skills will need to be covered before assigning a writing task. Preparation is the key to guiding students to successfully handle reading and writing tasks.

There are a few issues to be determined prior to teaching reading and writing in a class. For example, what role will reading and writing play in the class? What level(s) are your students in terms of reading and writing? What is the language background of your students? For example, do they use a Roman alphabet like English or a different system? Are they literate in their first language?

Role of Reading and Writing

Reading and writing play a primary role in an academic-style class but a lesser role in a conversational English class. Still, these skills should be incorporated to some degree in any ESL class. Even in a beginning-level conversational class students should learn how to write their names and addresses and to read simple English signs, such as "Stop" and "Danger." In an academic class students should be taught how to recognize and produce different genres of reading and writing. Those students who are preparing for university classes need to be taught how to read and write academic essays and research papers. A course designed for them would have to cover such topics as the use of a dictionary, encyclopedia, library card catalog, etc. In addition, teachers should address how to write an outline and bibliography, as well as the differences in citation styles.

Knowing the Levels of Your Students

Another vital area of preparation involves awareness of the reading and writing levels of your students. This initial assessment can occur during your program's registration day or on the first day of class. Reading can be tested by assigning a short text passage with some follow-up comprehension questions. Students can either write down the answers or respond verbally. If you want to differentiate, for example, where students fall on a spectrum of "low beginner" to "high intermediate," you may want to offer a series of increasingly difficult passages.

Another test to help assess both reading and writing proficiency is presenting a passage with blanks representing several missing words and then placing students according to the number/percentage they are able to fill in correctly. Intermediate-level students may determine the correct root word but add a wrong ending or include no ending at all (e.g., "He walk to the store" instead of "He walked to the store"). Reading and writing proficiency can also be assessed by asking students to fill out a registration form. If they can read the form and fill out the questions adequately, they are obviously at a higher level than those who cannot manage to read the directions and write down basic information like their name.

Language Background

The registration period is also a good time to determine what kind of background students have in terms of language learning. For example, are they able to read and write in their first language? Do they know the Roman alphabet even if their first language uses a different alphabet, such as the Arabic or Cyrillic script? If students do not know the Roman alphabet, you will need to begin teaching the ABCs right away. Have students learn to recognize the letters; repeat them aloud; and, most importantly, use them in words. It is important for retention to have students learn the alphabet in context. Students can also learn to write the alphabet, along with words containing those letters.

The English alphabet is notoriously difficult, even for those students who share the common Roman alphabet, such as Spanish speakers. Many English letters do not have a one-to-one correspondence to English sounds. For example, the sound we commonly spell with the letter "f" can also be spelled with "ph" as in *phone*, "gh" as in *rough* and "ff" as in *stuff.* Vowels open an even bigger can of worms! Consider the different sounds that are represented by the letter "o" in the following words: *women, robe,* and *bottle.* Every English teacher faces the moment when a student asks why the "o" is pronounced differently between *woman* and *women* and between *rob* and *robe*. In these situations, it is ok to say "I don't know!" There is, of course, always a phonetic or etymological answer, but it is best not to confuse your students with a technical response. A safe—and accurate—response is that English is a messy language!

First Language Literacy

As mentioned, it is also important to know whether or not students are literate in their first language. If not, you will have to progress very slowly in helping them gain proficiency in English. There is a big difference between working with international graduate students at a local university and teaching local migrant workers. Your determination of literacy level will also direct your class preparation in terms of what kinds of texts you will use. For a group of graduate students a book such as Josh McDowell's *More than a Carpenter*[1] might generate a fruitful discussion about Jesus, whereas a survival English class might better focus on reading signs and short passages.

Your ESL toolbox can be adapted to help you teach reading and writing in your classes. You should include an ESL dictionary—a dictionary written in English with simplified definitions and focusing on common words. Good examples, such as Heinle Publishers' *Newbury House Dictionary of American English*[2] and Longman's *Dictionary of American English*,[3] include an audio CD so that students can hear how the words are pronounced.

If you know the native languages of your students, you can also make use of one or more English/foreign-language dictionaries to help you explain particular concepts or words to your students. For example, you could use a Spanish-English dictionary to help a native Spanish speaker understand English words in a reading passage. Also include some easy reader stories or picture books, depending on the level you are teaching. If you are teaching the English alphabet, you should include alphabet flashcards, possibly including also both pictures and words. Instead of buying flashcards, you may want to make them using 3 x 5 note cards. Include a package of blank note cards in order to make up flashcards during a class session. Magnetic alphabet letters can be used to teach the alphabet.

Understand a Student's Attitude

A discussion of conversational English classes was included in Chapter 4. If students are expecting to take a conversational English class, they may not want to spend a lot of time covering reading and writing. Many students in conversational English classes already have a strong background in English grammar but desire to talk and communicate more fluently in English, especially with native speakers. On the other hand, students who sign up for an academic English class should expect to cover plenty of reading, writing, and grammar. Students who take an English class to prepare for a proficiency exam like the TOEFL (Test of English as a Foreign Language) will need to have a grasp of English grammar and know how to read and interpret the exam questions.

Another key aspect in gauging a student's attitude has to do with their reaction to any class time you spend promoting the Christian faith or discussing overtly Christian themes. Is this intended to be the primary emphasis of your program? If so, are students aware of this in advance? Some students may be highly skeptical of your teaching ability or agenda if they are afraid of being proselytized. As discussed in Chapter 1, we need to be ethical both in our promotion and in our teaching. If you advertise academic English classes to help with pronunciation, that is what you need to provide.

How you handle the overt presentation of biblical themes and the gospel message may also differ depending on whether you are teaching in the US or abroad. This issue will be fleshed out in Chapter 6. The main point here is that some students will not appreciate or even tolerate your using the Bible in class, possibly opting against continued involvement, while others will be open—or at least not adverse—to this approach. Some ESL classes are explicitly offered as discipleship or seekers' classes. Such classes are likely to attract Christians or those open to Christianity, resulting in a markedly different dynamic. Many students understand that if a class is offered in a church they should expect a Christian emphasis.

Encourage Students to Be Diligent Learners

We have discussed the importance for students of being diligent learners even outside the classroom in order to progress in their language proficiency. Teachers can help by providing regular homework activities. It is easier to assign reading and writing homework assignments, since these can both be done independently by the student.

The benefits of extensive reading for learning a language were covered in Chapter 2. It cannot be stressed enough how important it is for students to read regularly outside of class. Any kind of reading material is helpful, but it should be something that is enjoyable for the students so they will be motivated to continue doing it. One way to help your students is to provide a reading list and then to offer a prize or reward for completion. It is important as well to include a writing component, such as asking them to write a book report on each book or just on their favorite book. Another idea is to assign an oral book report or to conduct a less formal "show and tell" in response to books they have read. Even beginning-level readers can read picture books by themselves or aloud to the class. Everyone enjoys a good story! If appropriate English books are scarce because of geographic location or budget, you may have to create a lending library for your students. If you are near a public library, encourage your students to check out books from there.

Another way to help your students with reading homework is to provide a study guide for the book they are reading. This is especially helpful if the whole class is reading the same book. If the original edition is difficult to read, students may prefer an easy-reader version of the book if it is available.

The study of English grammar can be a long and arduous task. The best practice for understanding English grammar is extensive reading. The student will become familiar with seeing grammatical English in print and after a time will internalize the principles. Grammar is especially difficult to learn if it is presented only as a list of rules to be memorized by a student. While memorization is a part of learning grammar, it should never be the primary focus. Every ESL teacher needs a grammar book to help prepare lessons and to facilitate answering the inevitable question from students as to why some aspect of English grammar functions as it does. A good reference book, such as Richard Firsten's *The ELT Grammar Book*,[4] is recommended for those preparing formal lessons, while a smaller book, such as Raymond Murphy's *Basic Grammar in Use*,[5] is helpful for all teachers, especially those packing light for a short-term missions trip.

When we teach English we are to some degree automatically teaching grammar—the study of how the language is structured or put together. When people advocate that teachers not "teach grammar," they are really saying that we must be careful to avoid focusing too much on grammatical labels, such as "gerund" and "participle," and working instead on getting students to communicate fluently in English without thinking too hard about those labels. Knowledge of grammatical labels is helpful for teachers in order for them to categorize and organize lesson topics, but the overt use of such labels can get in the way of student learning. Perhaps it is best for teachers to teach grammar "undercover" by aiding students in constructing meaningful sentences in English. It is important for teachers to have a grasp of English grammar or at least to know where to find needed information in a reference book. In some cases native speakers of English are surprised to find out that their students know more about grammatical categories and terminology than they do!

Teaching grammar really comes down to this: Teach your students to communicate well in English. They must be able to express themselves so that they are understood and to function in several different kinds of contexts. Throughout the process students *will* be learning English grammar. For example, they will know that to form a complete sentence in English they will need a subject and a predicate. Whether they ultimately know that the part of the sentence that includes the verb is the "predicate" doesn't really matter, but they must be able to construct coherent phrases and sentences. The "power tools" covered in Chapter 4 can also be used to teach grammar. For example, a TPR lesson can be used to teach English prepositions and prepositional phrases like *in, on*, or *next to*. In addition, bear in mind that Carolyn Graham has written a book, titled *Grammarchants*,[6] for teaching grammar in a fun and alternative manner.

Encourage Communication

Communication in a language classroom is all about the production of a language—the ability to speak and write the language. Although speaking and writing are the active parts of communication, listening and reading are important complementary pieces to the overall process.

Written Journals

Students can communicate in English through a written journal. As introduced in Chapter 2, a written journal can either be utilized in class or assigned as homework. Journal assignments can be very structured. Often ESL textbooks include questions to prompt students' journal writing. For example, students can answer questions or reflect on information presented in the text. For an unstructured journal assignment, students can write about anything they choose. Another idea is for students to use their journal to write new English words they have encountered during the course of their day. A student can compile a list of words to look up and define (or to ask you about later in class). Journal assignments do not need to be long, but students should be encouraged to write in their journals every day.

In a formal class journals should be turned in for a grade. They are extremely helpful in terms of providing the teacher with a good idea of how the students are progressing, as well as a natural venue for teacher feedback. Journals can be graded in various ways (e.g., according to whether the student has successfully completed the task, for grammatical correctness, or for overall clarity of writing). In an informal class you can choose whether or not to have students turn in their journals. You do not necessarily need to grade the journals for content but should keep track or whether or not students have completed the task.

Connecting Reading and Writing

Within an ESL classroom you can connect reading and writing assignments. For example, students can be given a short reading passage and asked to write a response. Or they can be given a list of words, phrases, or short statements to connect within a full story they construct (e.g., students may be given the words "boy," "dog," and "ball" and asked to write a short story using those words). An important connection between reading and writing occurs when the Bible is used in an ESL classroom. There are many implications of using the Bible in class, some of which will be discussed in Chapter 6. If you decide to do so, you will need to decide which version to use and determine how you will use the Bible in class.

Which Bible Version to Use

If you decide (or are expected) to use the Bible in your ESL class, you will have to decide on a version to use. Bible translations have been rated according to levels of reading difficulty, based on word choice and sentence length. Dr. Joan Dungey, who has done research on readability and Bible use in ESL classrooms,[7] has used the Fry Readability graph to calculate the reading level of common English Bible versions.[8] An example she uses relates to Mark 5:12. The King James Version (KJV)[9] reads "Rejoice and be exceeding glad: for great is your reward in heaven," while the International Children's Version (ICV)[10] uses two shorter sentences to read, "Be happy and glad. You have a great reward waiting for you in heaven." The KJV has a reading level of 8.5, which means that a student needs to be at an eighth-grade reading level (fifth month) in order to easily read the text. The ICV, on the other hand, is rated at a 3.9 reading level (third grade, ninth month). Table 1, below, lists reading levels for a few common Bible translations.

Table 1: Readability of Bible Versions, adapted from Dungey (1986)[11]

Bible Version (New Testament only)	**Reading Level**
King James (Authorized) Version	8.5
New American Standard Bible (NASB, 1960)	8.5
New King James Version (NKJV,1979)	8
New International Version (NIV,1978)	7.3
International Children's Version (ICV, 1978)	3.9
New International Readers' Version (NIrV, 1996)	3.6

Note that the New International Readers' Version (NIrV), originally written for children so that they could easily transition into the NIV, has been popularly used in many church-based ESL classes, especially in churches that primarily use the NIV in their services.

How the Bible Can Be Used in an ESL Class

The decision of which version to use in a class and how it to use it will be based on several issues. A regular Bible translation would probably not be appropriate for use in a low-level class, although an easy-reader children's Bible might work for such a situation. Another option for beginning and intermediate students is for students to read the Bible in their native languages and then assign discussion questions for them to answer in English, either through spoken or written responses. An entry in their journal, for example, might include reflecting on a devotional passage. As already indicated, other issues that need to be addressed are whether a student is literate in their native language and whether that language uses a different alphabet. Either way, it is imperative that you progress slowly and make certain your students can comprehend the words and the meaning of the passage.

Summary

The teaching of reading and writing can seem like an insurmountable challenge. Teachers need to work step-by-step to introduce new vocabulary and to help students to understand the context. Journal writing is a key tool for any ESL instruction, from a formal classroom setting to a one-on-one tutoring session. Using the Bible in class can be effective, but the approach must be carefully considered prior to implementation.

Notes

1 Josh McDowell. *More Than a Carpenter* (Tyndale House Publishers, 1987).

2 *Newbury House Dictionary of American English.* 4th ed. (Heinle Publishers, 2004).

3 *Dictionary of American English* (Longman Publishers, 2008).

4 Richard Firsten and Patricia Killan. *The ELT Grammar Book* (ALTA Books, 2002).

5 Raymond Murphy. *Basic Grammar in Use: Reference and Practice for Students of English* (Cambridge University Press, 1993).

6 Carolyn Graham. *Grammarchants* (Oxford University Press, 1993).

7 Joan M. Dungey. *Bible Studies for New English Speakers* (Seattle: Brim Press, 1986). See also Dungey and Worthington, "Readability and the Bible: Which Version for your Students?" *Christian Educators Journal*, Dec 85/Jan 86 and Joan M. Dungey, "Bible Readability: Which Bible Should I Use for My ESL Students?" www.eslbible.com/id15.html.

8 Edward Fry. *Elementary Reading Instruction* (New York: McGraw-Hill, 1977). Downloadable Fry Graphs can be accessed from the Discovery Education site at http://school.discovery.com/schrockguide/fry/html.

9 *The Holy Bible* (King James / Authorized Version) (Cambridge University Press, 1995).

10 *International Children's Version* (Word Publishing Group, 1978).

11 Dungey (1986). Can be accessed at www.eslbible.com/id15.html.

For Further Study

Folse, Keith S., and Betty Azar. *Keys to Teaching Grammar to English Language Learners: A Practical Handbook* (Ann Arbor, MI: University of Michigan Press, 2009).

Yule, George. *Explaining English Grammar (Oxford Handbooks for Language Teachers)* (Oxford: Oxford University Press, 1999).

Chapter 6

Connecting Contexts and Principles

Introduction

The subtitle of this book, *Contexts and Principles*, contains two important words, both of which are relevant on several levels and were deliberately chosen to reflect the main idea of this book. The introduction presented the three teaching contexts of formal classroom teaching, a short-term missions trip, and one-on-one tutoring through the stories of Jackie, Keith, and Carol. Chapter 1 described the principles that are foundational to an ESL ministry, while Chapter 2 discussed the teaching and learning principles relevant to an ESL classroom. These principles form the foundation of a "philosophy of teaching statement," which was explained in Chapter 3. Chapters 4 and 5 applied the principles within this statement to the areas of listening, speaking, reading, and writing. This final chapter will make further connections between contexts and principles. Overall, the content of this book has been presented and organized to answer the following question: *What does it look like to teach English in context?* When one succeeds in doing so, the results are effective teaching, effective learning, and, ultimately, an effective ministry.

Connecting Contexts and Principles

The proposition to "teach English in context" has many points of application, since we can look at the idea of "context" in several ways. One way in which we can identify three different kinds of contexts, as they are described in this book, is in using the terms *format*, *function*, and *field*.

Format as Context

Our first connection between context and principles can be seen within teaching *formats*. We have described three teaching contexts in particular: the formal classroom setting, a short-term missions trip, and one-on-one tutoring. In each of these formats teachers need to adapt and apply principles, as stated in a personal "philosophy of teaching statement." The concept of being principled applies to teaching formats, as has been described in detail in Chapters 1–5. In each context and situation a teacher is obligated to be prepared; excellence in teaching is simply not optional. A principled teacher is one who specifically prepares to teach within a particular context. This has been spelled out in the discussions of being ethical and being prepared to teach. Let's look at Jackie and Keith to see how they applied principles to their context formats.

Jackie's Story—Final Diary Entry from Her Short-Term Missions Trip

Jackie wrote the following entry as she was about to leave Asia after six weeks of teaching ESL to college-aged students:

I can't believe I'm leaving for home tomorrow! These last six weeks have been exhausting, but also so awesome! I have enjoyed bonding with the other teachers on our team and am going to miss meeting together every evening to talk about our day and see what worked from our lesson plans and what didn't. It helped so much that we were able to encourage each other and work to be really prepared for the next day's class. I want to definitely come back here next year. I need to ask our team leader, Mary, where I can get some more TESOL training. It will be so much better next year if I am that much more prepared!

Keith's Story—A Church Testimony

Keith was invited by his church's pastor to give a testimony about the ESL ministry. This is a little of what he shared with his church:

This year I began teaching in the ESL program here at church. I was pretty unsure of myself as a teacher, but I wanted to be involved in our outreach to the community. I have always been interested in learning about other cultures, so I was drawn to taking part in the ESL ministry. I am so thankful for the direction that Pastor and others gave me to attend some training workshops before starting to teach. I wanted to see two things happen—that my students would be more confident in speaking English and that they would be open to hearing about Christ. Juan started attending ESL classes this year. I was so excited when he began attending class, and I prayed that he would stay in the class. He was pretty faithful in attending, and one night after class he stayed to talk. He thanked me for teaching him English. He appreciated our church for offering a quality program. It meant so much to him. He opened his heart to Christ that night because of the love that was displayed in our church. Praise the Lord! I am so excited about this ministry. I can't wait for classes to begin again in a few weeks . . .

Function as Context

We have also seen the idea of context coming up in the discussion of using a communicative approach to teaching English (e.g., what is the *function* of English?). English learners should know how to speak English in different circumstances, such as how to talk with a grocery store clerk as opposed to using English in a job interview. The goal of the English language learner is to be *communicatively competent* in English and able to successfully use the language in a variety of real-life situations. Language learning should be practical and ultimately beneficial to the learner.

An important ESL teaching and learning principle covered in Chapter 2 is that we want to see our students *communicate.* We saw how we can help them to communicate silently, with gestures, at the beginning and then gradually encourage them to speak with ever-increasing confidence. The chapter also stressed that English should be taught in context so that students can remember the language better. Language learning is more than just memorizing lists of words; it is learning how to communicate effectively in different situations. We want to see our students being able to adjust, compensate, and excel in the variety of social contexts they will encounter. As teachers, we can prepare lessons that will expose our students to different social contexts. Carol shares one such instance in a letter she sent to a friend.

Carol's Story—Teaching Her Neighbor about Parent-Teacher Conferences

You may remember that I have been meeting with my neighbor Rosa to help her learn English. She was anxious about being prepared for conferences with her children's teachers. We spent some time going over report cards, and I helped explain some terms she needed to know about school. I even played the role of a teacher and helped prepare Rosa for speaking with her kids' teachers. It was kind of fun, but it also helped her feel more confident about what to expect in a parent-teacher conference. …

Keith's Story—Teaching Adult ESL Students about Driving Laws

Helping students communicate within specific contexts can be done within any format. For example, Keith's church has an annual driving school for its ESL learners, to which it invites a local police officer to speak about driving laws. Keith shares how this program helped his adult ESL students:

Ivan attended our driver's training day and was so thankful for the information. He was able to learn about the different driving laws and how to read signs in English. He feels confident now that he can pass the driving test. He was also so glad that Officer Mitchell from the local police department shared with the group. One intimidating situation faced by many adults from other countries is being pulled over by a police officer. Ivan learned some life-saving tips (such as the importance of staying in the vehicle) and came away from the session much less anxious. It was helpful for him to be reminded that things work differently in our country and that police officers here don't take bribes! ...

Field as Context

A third way to "teach English in context" is to display sensitivity in your lesson preparation. A teacher must always be aware of the host culture and teaching customs. If you are teaching in the US, this translates into an awareness of and sensitivity to the culture and customs of each student's country of origin. The way things are done in typical American classrooms may not be successful or even appropriate in other situations. The country or *field* in which one teaches can and must greatly influence the approach in an ESL class. There are three important aspects for a teacher to keep in mind: A teacher needs (1) to always continue to be a learner, (2) to be culturally sensitive, and (3) to affirm a student's identity in the classroom.

The Teacher as Learner

The least effective kind of teacher is one who believes he or she knows everything. The best teachers, on the other hand, are those who approach their task with a healthy dose of humility. Cross-cultural travel can bring out both responses in a person. Those who travel may wonder *why* people do things so strangely in the host country and may reason that the ways we do them here in the West are intrinsically better. Culture shock can cause us to become highly critical of cultural differences. There are also many situations in which functioning within another culture can be very humbling. Trying to pronounce simple sentences like "Where is the bathroom?" can be extremely difficult if one does not know the language well.

When you travel to another culture as a teacher, it is imperative that you ask questions rather than assuming either that the people in the host country do things the same way we do here or that the way we do things in the West is necessarily better. A teacher must be an active learner. Learn about the host country and its educational system. What are the schools like? Do most children go to school? What are the classrooms like? Do all students stand when the teacher enters the room? How do students address teachers in this society? Do students call their teachers by their first names or by a title like "professor"?

A key question relates to classroom methodology and pedagogy. How are students taught in this country? For example, is rote memorization stressed? What do people perceive as the primary role of the teacher—to disseminate information or to facilitate learning? While we are invariably shaped by our own educational paths, we also gravitate to those learning styles with which we ourselves are most comfortable and, as teachers, are drawn toward teaching in the way we learned best. This tendency is especially important to recognize for those of us who have received formal educational training. We in particular may be prone to assuming that the way things are done in the West is necessarily best.

It is wise for a teacher in this situation to do some background research ahead of time to find out what the schools are like. Talk with your contact in the country, if you have one, to glean information. If possible once you've reached your destination, take time to observe the school and the class to get a feel for how things are done in the school.

Jackie's Missions Trip Preparation

Before Jackie traveled to Asia with her team, she learned that the classes in her host culture are formal, with students sitting behind desks in straight rows. Her students would wear uniforms to class and address her as "Teacher" or "Miss Smith." It would take some time for Jackie, who was accustomed to professors who dressed casually and addressed students on a first-name basis, inviting them to do the same, to get used to students who were almost her own age treating her with a detached respect. Her college instructors tended to be very informal, at times sharing jokes before class and even throwing pens to awaken sleeping students. Her classroom in Asia, in contrast, seemed "old fashioned" and strange.

Jackie had learned in advance that neither classroom situation is necessarily "right" or "wrong" but that different cultures may have markedly different expectations for the educational experience. It must be said, however, that a teacher can sensitively introduce some new ways of doing things. For example, Jackie did introduce her class to some group work and role-playing tasks, neither of which was normally done in that school. She was careful in the process, however, to choose culturally appropriate topics and activities.

Teachers Learning the Host Language

As we have discussed, it is also important for a teacher to learn at least some rudiments of the language of the host country. Even if you will be traveling for only a few weeks, it is important for you to learn a few key words and phrases in that language. This can be of practical help, but more importantly it shows that you are interested in and respectful of that culture and its people. As we saw in Chapter 1, when Carol learned a little Spanish she found that this opened up her relationship with her neighbor Rosa. It is so important for an ESL teacher to have gone through the experience of learning a second language. Cross-cultural missionaries can be great ESL teachers because they themselves have gone through the process of struggling within another language and culture. That experience can prepare them to commiserate with their ESL students and encourage them to do well.

Cultural Sensitivity

In what areas do we need to be culturally sensitive as teachers? We have seen that a general awareness of teaching and learning styles is important when teaching cross-culturally. Another key aspect is the choice of curriculum and textbooks. Most ESL textbooks—and that includes many good ones—are heavily influenced by American or British culture. These textbooks may work very well in an ESL class in the US or England but may not be as effective in other countries. For example, a picture of a young man and woman to accompany a story about friends in school may unintentionally reflect immoral connotations for learners within that culture.

Language and culture are intrinsically linked, but it is still vital for teachers to recognize that English is not "owned" by the US, England, or any other country that happens to espouse it as its official language. The English language is used by millions of people worldwide, and we need to accept the fact that varieties such as "Indian English" and "West African English" lay claim to the language just as legitimately as any American, Canadian, or British manner of speaking. The result is a concept that has come to be called "World English"—an international variety of English that does not necessarily lean toward the US or Britain but acknowledges the fact that millions of people speak and use English away from the old colonial centers.

There is a debate raging in the field of TESOL between those who see the spread of English worldwide as a positive result of globalization and others who negatively perceive this trend, viewing it as a form of linguistic imperialism.[1] While the imperialism debate is outside the scope of this volume, we do well to realize that the goal of English teachers should not be to make English students into Americans or Britons. The goal is to help students become proficient in English within their own cultural context. English students in India should learn to become proficient in the English used in India, those in Kenya should learn the Kenyan variety, and so on. Cultural identity should be maintained rather than eliminated by the acquisition of English.

Affirming Identity

Finally, we need to affirm the identity of our students. Individual identities are inextricably bound to language and culture.

When someone learns a second language, that person is vulnerable to undergoing a minor "identity crisis." The goal of English language classes should be what is called "additive bilingualism"[2]—ideally, we will see students becoming more proficient in *both* languages. This should also be the case with regard to language instruction within English-speaking countries. Schools in the US should embrace policies that help promote a student's heritage language in addition to English, as opposed to attempting to replace a student's heritage language with English. In the broader scheme of things, ESL teachers should not support measures that would lead to the elimination of indigenous languages. English globalization should not come at the expense of other languages.

Jackie's Class Project—English Book Reports

Jackie wanted to see her students succeed in both English and Thai, their native language. She had originally intended to use in class an English-language book that contained short stories about English nursery rhymes. Instead, she encouraged her students to read a local author her missionary host had recommended. She herself found an English translation of the book to familiarize herself with the plot and themes. She then asked her students to write a book report in English, followed up with oral reports on the book, again in English. This activity promoted the students' engagement with readings in their mother tongue while also promoting English proficiency. This kind of project can also be done in the US. All students can read the same book, each in their own language, after which they can work in groups or individually to prepare a class presentation in English.

English-Only Rules in Class

Another issue to consider is whether or not you will have an "English-only" rule for your classroom. This kind of rule is often (wearily) enforced in a classroom to promote communication in English. It may work well with advanced-level students but is ineffective in lower-level classes. First, students do not have a sufficient grasp of the language to communicate successfully in all situations. Second, the intention may backfire, with the result that students do not communicate at all. You may decide to impose a limited English-use rule within prescribed situations, such as asking for permission to leave class and the like.

In my opinion, however, a better approach is to allow your students to use their first language in class. Encourage them, in fact, to use their native languages in group work in order to accomplish a task. If your students tend not to stay on task, you may need to monitor the situation, but in general allowing and even encouraging the use of their first language can help beginning-level students. Affirming their identities is an important way in which you as the teacher can show respect to individual students, their language, and their culture.

Keith's ESL Class—Culture Day

Keith's ESL class hosts an annual culture day at the church. Students bring in items and foods representing their home cultures and take turns (in English) explaining the different items and teaching the other students some words and phrases from their native language. This is a great way for students to come to respect and appreciate each other's diverse cultures. You may also want to participate in explaining customs and traditions from your home state or country. Holidays are a great time to talk about traditions, many of which, such as Christmas and Easter, have overtly Christian themes.

Conclusion

The task of "teaching English in context" can be accomplished if you follow the principles set forth in this book. This can be done in such a way as to result in effective teaching, effective learning, and ultimately an effective ministry.

Notes

1 For a deeper look at the globalism-imperialism debate, read David Crystal's *English as a Global Language*, 2nd ed. (Cambridge University Press, 2003) to see how the spread of English is seen in a positive light. Then read Robert Phillipson's *Linguistic Imperialism* (Oxford University Press, 1992) for an explanation of how the spread of English is viewed as damaging.

2 See Colin Baker's *Foundations of Bilingual Education and Bilingualism*, 4th ed. (Multilingual Matters, 2006) for a good description of bilingualism and bilingual education.

For Further Study

Livermore, David. *Serving with Eyes Wide Open: Doing Short-Term Missions with Cultural Intelligence* (Grand Rapids, MI: Baker Books, 2006).

———. *Cultural Intelligence: Improving your CQ to Engage our Multicultural World* (Grand Rapids, MI: Baker Academic, 2009).

Canagarajah, A. Suresh. *Resisting Linguistic Imperialism* (Cambridge University Press, 1999).

Appendix A

ESL Ministry Set-Up Checklist

The following are steps to consider when preparing to start or continue an ESL outreach ministry at your church or ministry.

	Assemble *ESL ministry planning team* (ideally 5 to 8, including representatives from outreach or missions team and pastoral staff).
	Each planning team member should read *An ESL Ministry Handbook* (especially the introduction and Chapters 1–3) before the first planning meeting.
	Gather *demographic information.* • What is the neighborhood around your church like? • Who is your target student group? • Will you focus on "adopting" one people group with which to work? • Will you partner with a sister church (such as a Hispanic or Korean church)? • Or will you work with a diverse population of students representing your area?

	Construct a *mission / goal statement* for your program (see Chapter 3 for guidance).
	Teachers develop their own *personal philosophy of mission statements* (see Chapter 3) in conjunction with the program goals.
	Decide *when and how often you will hold ESL classes* (take student as well as teacher considerations into account). • Consider transportation needs. • Consider childcare options (e.g., have a baby-sitter at the church?). • Consider whether to hold ESL classes in conjuction with other church ministries, such as mid-week children's ministries (to capitalize on built-in child care, transportation, meals, etc.).
	Find *classroom space.* • Will you have more than one class (e.g., divided by level or gender)? • Will you hold the class at the church or some other location? • Is the designated space set up well for classroom use (e.g., are there enough chairs, sufficient lighting, a white board, etc.?)? • Consider rent/utilities costs.

	Choose *a curriculum* to use. • The curriculum should align with your program mission/goal. • It should meet the needs of your student population (e.g., survival English vs. academic English, etc.). • Ask publishers for free exam copies of texts.
	Set your *budget* (see Appendix B).
	Set *teacher training* times. • Initial training for teachers in the program. • Ongoing development training (e.g., ESL conferences, hosting special speakers, etc.).
	Set *registration day* for students. • Advertise (at church, in the community, etc.). • Prepare placement testing (see Appendix C). • Prepare (and translate?) registration forms (see Appendix D). • Set calendar (e.g., start, end, breaks, parties and other special events, etc.).
	Prepare for *first day of class.* • Teachers and tutors assigned. • Materials ordered and ready. • Classroom set and prepared.
	Pray!

Appendix B

ESL Ministry Budget Checklist

The budget for an ESL ministry can vary depending on a variety of factors. This checklist will give you a sense of possible costs to consider as you are planning to start an ESL ministry.

Startup Costs

	Advertising (e.g., printing costs, ads in newspaper, website design, sign, etc.)
	Reference materials (e.g., ESL dictionaries, foreign-language dictionaries, ESL reference books for lesson and activity ideas)
	Classroom materials • Whiteboards (and easel) • Tables and chairs
	Computers • Hardware • Software (e.g., language programs such as *Rosetta Stone*)

Ongoing Costs

	Classroom space • Rent • Utilities
	Curriculum (e.g., full cost covered by program, partial cost covered by students; full cost covered by students) • Videos/DVDs • Online subscriptions (e.g., for lesson planning sites, etc.) • Supplemental materials (e.g., foreign language Bibles, tracts, etc.)
	Office expenses • Postage • Photocopying • Classroom supplies (e.g., pens, markers, etc.) • Certificates (e.g., for unit completion or end-of-year ceremony) • Internet access
	Hospitality expenses • Coffee • Snacks • Paperware (e.g., cups, plates, napkins, etc.) • Party/activity expenses (e.g., decorations, gifts, etc.)

	Transportation expenses (e.g., gas, travel expenses)
	Teacher Development • Honorarium for guest speakers • Registration fees for ESL workshops and conferences • Membership fees for organizations such as TESOL or the Christian English Language Educators Association (CELEA)

Appendix C

Placement Testing

Chapter 4 stressed the need to test students in all skill areas. For example, a student may do well conversing with others but struggle with reading and writing. On the other hand, you may have a student who has a difficult time communicating with others verbally but is strong in reading and grammar. You don't need expensive and lengthy assessment tests. Here are a few guidelines to follow to get a snapshot view of the level of your ESL students. For a more complete version of the oral and written assessment tests, see Susan Burke's excellent guide *ESL: Creating a Quality English as a Second Language Program* (1998, CRC Publications).

Speaking (includes oral and listening skills and pronunciation):

You can divide students into *beginning/intermediate/advanced* groups based on short conversations. Briefly, if students have difficulty answering basic questions, they would be assigned to the beginning level. If they can understand the questions and give short answers (can use complete sentences without much elaboration), they could be placed in the intermediate level. Students who can sustain a conversation and delve into deeper topics would be assigned to the advanced level. Burke (1998) delves into these levels a bit more deeply and provides numerical placement criteria as well.

Writing (includes grammar and writing):

If students have had English classes in their home country, they may have a higher writing/grammar placement than would be evident from their speech. However, if students have learned English in a more communicative setting or through immersion in an English-speaking country, their speaking may be at a higher level than their reading/writing.

You can determine whether students are at a beginning, intermediate, or advanced level in other ways as well. For example, you can give a writing prompt, such as asking about their day or their thoughts on a particular current event. You would grade their responses much as you would those for the speaking section, above. If they are unable to write anything, they would be in the low-beginning level. If they can write a few words and phrases, they would be classified either as high-beginner or low-intermediate. If they are able to write simple sentences, they may be considered high-intermediate. Advanced students would be able to elaborate and write longer sentences.

Second, you can use an exercise such as that found in Burke (1998), which uses a story with blanks. The student needs to fill in the blanks with words that make sense in the story. The number of mistakes is added up to determine the proficiency level of the student. This kind of exercise would also test the student's reading ability.

Reading (includes writing):

You can test the reading proficiency of students by assigning them a short reading passage. You may find that your student has limited reading proficiency in their native language or that their native language uses a different writing system than the Roman script of English. Based on such criteria, you may place those students at a *preliteracy* level to help them write the alphabet and learn to spell in English.

Appendix D

Sample Registration Form

Name: ______________________________________

Address: ____________________________________

Telephone/Cell Number(s): ___________________

E-mail: ______________________________________

Native Country/Language: ____________________

Questions:

1. How long have you been in the US?

2. Are you a student in school?

3. Do you work outside of the home?

4. Why do you want to learn English?
   - ☐ I need more English to get a job.
   - ☐ I need more English to speak or write better at my job.

- ☐ I want to make friends with Americans.
- ☐ I want to speak English so I can help my children in school.
- ☐ I want to get around the community better (shopping, appointments, etc.).
- ☐ I want to study in a college or university in the future.
- ☐ I need help with my homework from school.
- ☐ I want to improve my English skills in general.
- ☐ Other. (Please explain).

5. What are you most interested in learning?
   - ☐ Life skills (how to get around the city)
   - ☐ Vocabulary (learning new English words)
   - ☐ Writing in English
   - ☐ English grammar
   - ☐ Listening
   - ☐ Having a conversation in English
   - ☐ English pronunciation
   - ☐ Reading in English

6. How did you hear about our English classes?

Appendix E

Sample Advertising Flyer

English

English Classes

Work on Your English Skills:

Conversation, Pronunciation, Listening, Reading, and Writing

Registration:

Wednesday, September 3, 2011, at 6:30 p.m.

Cost:

Classes are free. Students buy their own books.

Classes: (Starting September 10)

Wednesdays 6:30–8:00 p.m.

(Morning classes will also be held if needed.)

If you have questions, please call (616) 555-1212

English Language Classes

First Baptist Church

[Church Address]

www.churchwebaddress/esl.org

[Include a map to your church]

Appendix F

Sample Advertising Flyer

Spanish

¡Clases de inglés!

Mejore su inglés:

Conversación, Pronunciación, Lectura, y Escritura

Inscribimos estudiantes nuevos el miércoles 3 de septiembre.

Las clases comienzan el miércoles 10 de septiembre.

(También habrá clases por la mañana si hay interés.)

Horario:

Las clases se reúnen los miércoles por la tarde (6:30-8:00 p.m.)

(También habrá clases por la mañana si hay interés.)

Precio:

¡Las clases son gratis! Usted puede comprar su propio libro de texto.

Si necesita más información, llame al (616) 555-1212.

English Language Classes

First Baptist Church

[Church Address]

www.churchwebaddress/esl.org

[Include a map to your church]